Jonas Teixeira Marinho

Amnesty in Brazil and Argentina

Jonas Teixeira Marinho

Amnesty in Brazil and Argentina

An international analysis

ScienciaScripts

Imprint

Cover image: www.ingimage.com

This book is a translation from the original published under ISBN 978-3-330-19760-2.

Publisher:
Sciencia Scripts
is a trademark of
Dodo Books Indian Ocean Ltd. and OmniScriptum S.R.L publishing group

120 High Road, East Finchley, London, N2 9ED, United Kingdom
Str. Armeneasca 28/1, office 1, Chisinau MD-2012, Republic of Moldova, Europe
Printed at: see last page
ISBN: 978-620-8-23889-6

To my parents.

ACKNOWLEDGMENTS

First of all, I must thank God for giving me the gift of life and for giving me the confidence to pursue my goals, however difficult they may be.

To my mother, Rosivalda, for her unconditional love, emotional support and encouragement to read, not just while writing this book, but at every stage of my life. To my father, Jarbas, for always encouraging me to pursue professional challenges.

To my brother, Matheus, for the precious moments of silence and understanding while I was working on this project. Rita, who since childhood has always kept the environment clean and always tried to ensure the tranquillity necessary for intellectual exercise.

To my cousin Rodrigo, for encouraging me and helping me with tips on the work. To my aunt Rosalba, for praying for me in my time of need.

To Professor Marcio Diniz, who, from the time of my internship at PGM, contributed to my intellectual enrichment. He also emphasized the importance of research and determination, and opened my eyes to various academic opportunities. I also discussed various texts with him on different subjects. I would also like to thank him for his willingness to guide me in the preparation of this book, even before I knew the subject in detail.

Finally, to my undergraduate and specialization colleagues, especially Candice, Francisca, Rodrigo, Victor, Kate, Tiago, Rafael, Nairim, Sara and Cyntia, for being good friends and for helping and encouraging me on my long road to professional success.

I would also like to thank Novas Edigoes Academicas for believing in the potential of this work.

"We swallow at once the lie that flatters us and drink drop by drop the truth that embittered us." (Denis Diderot)

SUMMARY

INTRODUCTION

Amnesty in the context of transitional justice is one of the most thought-provoking topics in the legal debate today. There is no denying that the discussion is really interesting, with good arguments on both sides of the debate. Studies related to amnesty, however, have many limitations, as they only focus on the arguments in favor or against this form of transition within a specific state.

We therefore need an analysis that goes beyond traditional arguments and seeks to understand amnesty in a broader context, understanding the repercussions it has had on the international community and the influences it exerts on states to make certain decisions regarding the transition to democracy.

This paper aims to study not only the arguments used by the parties in the debate, but in what context they arise, as well as the respective influences that steer the discussion towards one side or the other.

In today's society, it is impossible to study certain phenomena without considering the interactions between states and the international commitments made by representatives of those states. Amnesty is one of these phenomena, since the strengthening of international human rights law makes any debate on amnesty that disregards the development of the issue on the international stage incomplete and poor.

In order to achieve the objective of this work, which is to understand the reasons why Brazil and Argentina have completely divergent positions on amnesty and to study amnesty more broadly, it is essential to know some theories of historical science.

Most amnesties in Latin America took place in the late 1970s and 1980s. Any analysis that disregards the historical context in which the laws were enacted is therefore incomplete. Furthermore, it is not enough to know the historical context through classic historicist theories. It is essential to consider the latest advances in historiography in order to apply the historiographical current that best fits the object of study.

It is now important to present how the ideas will be distributed, so that the reader understands the objective and methodology of this work. In Chapter 1, the reader will be introduced to the traditional and recent schools of the study of history. This presentation is necessary for the focus of the research to be understood. Chapter 2 discusses amnesty in Brazil. Because of its specificities, in chapter 3 I will comment on amnesty in Argentina.

Chapter 1 provides an overview of the evolution of historiographical thought, starting with the History of Concepts, traditional in German doctrine, and going through an important debate between the Cambridge school and the conceptualists.

Next, Joao Feres Junior's ambitious project to build a conceptual history of Brazil is presented. After analyzing these historiographical currents, historians detected some flaws. Therefore, the theory of Global History was proposed, in order to study history over a wider spatial and temporal range. Finally, we analyze the possibility of applying the theory of Global History to the study of amnesty, and the application of conceptual history to some fundamental terms in the discussion about the transition to democracy.

Chapter 2 focuses on amnesty in Brazil. The study begins with the historical context, since it is necessary to understand the Brazilian dictatorship and the moment in which the Amnesty Law was enacted. The historical study is not limited to the classic understanding of traditional history, but establishes links with the world situation, which had a clear influence on the 1964 coup and the repression of opponents.

This is followed by a presentation of the concept of transitional justice and an analysis of which model of transitional justice Brazil is affiliated with. A third point focuses on the incompatibility of the Amnesty Law with international law. Because it contravenes various international principles and conventions, the Brazilian law has been severely criticized by internationalists. Finally, the chapter concludes with the controversial decision of the Federal Supreme Court, which ruled that the Amnesty Law was constitutional.

Having gone through a similar process of military dictatorship, having amnesty laws that have been criticized by international law scholars and having reached a final decision through its Supreme Court, in chapter 3 the methodology is the same as in chapter 2.

This final chapter analyzes amnesty in Argentina. A comprehensive study of Argentine history in the 20th century is carried out, since the study of the military period alone is insufficient to understand the development of the Argentine transitional justice system.

Next, we look at how Argentina's transitional justice has varied from movements towards impunity to, at present, accountability for the agents who committed human rights violations under the regime of exception. The question of the incompatibility of Argentina's two amnesty laws with international law is discussed below.

Finally, we analyze the decision of the *Supreme Court of Justice of the Nation,* which decided to declare the amnesty laws unconstitutional, using international conventions ratified by Argentina and the idea of *jus cogens.*

It is hoped that, after reading this work, the reader will have a more comprehensive view of amnesty, understanding the international and not just national debate on the subject, as well as having an opinion formulated through legal arguments, disregarding the media debate on the subject.

Finally, this work aims to contribute to research into justiga de transigao and to draw the attention of Brazilian society to the relevance of the issue, which is not only in the past, but has serious implications in contemporary Brazil, especially with the rise of extreme right-wing figures who aim to minimize the suffering of the victims of the military regime.

1 FROM CONCEPTUAL HISTORY TO GLOBAL HISTORY

1.1 Origins of Conceptual History

Conceptual history emerged in Germany through the work *Begriffsgeschichte*, written by Reinhart Koselleck. This school proposes a revision of the method by which historical science is studied. In order to understand a historical phenomenon, one must use the paradigm of the place of speech, i.e. study the fundamental concepts in force at the time with the meaning attributed to them by various social actors.

Initially, Koselleck's ideas were strongly influenced by the famous jurist Carl Schmitt, with whom he maintained close contact, including through an exchange of letters. His early work could be seen as a dialogue with Schmitt's work[1] . Over time, however, there was a gradual distancing between Koselleck's work and Schmitt's ideas.

The method established by the *Begriffsgeschichte* can be applied to any historical period and any community of speakers of a language .[2] Currently, there are several conceptual history projects around the world, including in Brazil (see section 1.3). The success of the conceptual history method lies in its innovative and more comprehensive analysis of the reality of certain historical periods.

Conceptual history is also concerned with moments of continuity and rupture, analyzing how concepts fell into disuse, how they were transformed or how, even after important historical changes, they managed to retain their original meaning. In this context, it is essential to understand the scope of the term *Sattelzeit*, which represents the period from 1750 to 1850, corresponding to the transition between the beginning of modernity and modernity itself in Germany. This period is considered by

---

[1] SEBASTIAN, Javier Fernandez. Contra la historia (en singular). An interpretation of the work of Reinhart Koselleck. **Ariadna historica. Lenguajes, conceptos, metaforas**, Bilbao, v. 1, 2012. p. 251.

[2] FERES JUNIOR, Joao. Towards a critical conceptual history of Brazil: welcoming the *Begriffgeschichte.* In: FERES JUNIOR, Joao (org.); JASMIN, Marcelo (org.). **Historia dos conceitos**: dialogos transatlanticos. Rio de Janeiro: PUC Rio, Loyola, IUPERJ, 2007, p. 110.

Koselleck to be fundamental in the history of humanity, as it caused the break between the archaic and modernity.

The notion of *Sattelzeit* as a fundamental concept, however, is not immune to criticism. Frangois-Xavier Guerra states that it is impossible to consider that the period between 1750-1850 was the only time when there was a significant conceptual change. Furthermore, it is impossible to consider that tradition and modernity are completely antagonistic blocks, with clear, homogeneous and coherent delimitations[3].

The process of conceptual change is complex and usually occurs when there is a major rupture in society. Transformation, however, can occur without there being a rupture, because a concept restricted to the academic sphere can become popularized and lose its original meaning or a vulgar concept can be refined and given a theoretical explanation .[4]

According to Koselleck, some concepts are basic, i.e. indispensable for formulating the urgent questions of a certain historical period. Basic concepts are irreplaceable components of a people's political and social vocabulary. To be considered a basic political concept, a concept must be contested, have a long history, often produce unforeseen political consequences and also be used by the media[5]. Basic concepts include freedom and democracy in the Western societies of the 20th century.

A fundamental concept in contemporary times is that of Republic. Considered by many to be the ideal form of government, the Republic takes on the role of a basic concept. Pocock has a particular definition of Republic, considering it not just as a set of ideas, but as a specific language.

The Republic, for Pocock, is not infinite and deals with the "Machiavellian moment", which represents the conceptual period in which it is confronted with its finitude, trying to remain morally and politically stable in a flow of events that destroy

---

[3] PALTI, Elias P. Temporality and refutability of political concepts. In: FERES JUNIOR, Joao (org.); JASMIN, Marcelo (org.). **Historia dos conceitos**: dialogos transatlanticos. Rio de Janeiro: PUC Rio, Loyola, IUPERJ, 2007, p. 63.

[4] PALONEN, Kari. Times of politics and conceptual temporalization: a new program for conceptual history. In: FERES JUNIOR, Joao (org.); JASMIN, Marcelo (org.). **Historia dos conceitos**: dialogos transatlanticos . Rio de Janeiro: PUC Rio, Loyola, IUPERJ, 2007, p. 35.

[5] RICHTER, Melvin. More than a two-way street: analyzing, translating and comparing political concepts from other cultures. In: FERES JUNIOR, Joao (org.); JASMIN, Marcelo (org.). **Historia dos conceitos**: dialogos transatlanticos. Rio de Janeiro: PUC Rio, Loyola, IUPERJ, 2007, p. 22.

the system of secular stability .[6]

Still on the republican question, the meaning of the right of insurrection is complex. For the government, rebels seek nothing more than to overthrow the regime, and are always subversives or vandals. For the rebels, the government violates rights. The right to rebel is guaranteed by law, but the insurrection seeks to violate the existing order. This contradiction has yet to find a satisfactory solution.

Another important issue arises when we make a comparative historical analysis. When comparing the meaning of concepts in different cultures, it must be taken into account that the process of translation ends up leading to an adaptation and loss of part of the meaning that the term would have in the other language. To really understand the meaning and scope of a concept, it is essential to study its historical evolution and its use in the most varied discourses in a society.

It can be seen from the brief considerations above that political concepts are indeterminate in their meaning, and can have a specific meaning for a certain group and mean something completely different for another group.

Political concepts can only have their meaning reconstructed in the analysis of a given historical period when the context is considered fundamental. The context of the debates in which concepts were constructed or used must be sought out by the historical researcher. The arguments for and against the meaning attributed to a concept by a particular group must be emphatically researched.

Conceptual history, therefore, is concerned not only with reconstructing concepts in a given society in a specific historical period. It also seeks to facilitate understanding of the controversies, ruptures and different meanings that a term can have in different societies.

1.2 Conceptual History and the Cambridge School

The Cambridge School is a counterpoint to conceptual history, presenting

---

6 POCOCK, J.G.A. The Machiavellian Moment. Princeton, 1975, p.8 *apud* PALTI, Elias P. Temporality and refutability of political concepts. In: FERES JUNIOR, Joao (org.); JASMIN, Marcelo (org.). **Historia dos conceitos**: dialogos transatlanticos. Rio de Janeiro: PUC Rio, Loyola, IUPERJ, 2007, p. 66.

another methodology for the study of history. It emerged in England and to this day is the dominant historiographical current in English-speaking countries. Its main exponents are John Pocock and Quentin Skinner.

The Cambridge School initially sought to break with the tradition of studying the history of ideas that had existed in England until the mid-20th century. In short, the historiography of ideas sought to understand historical phenomena through the study of facts, without taking historical agents into account.

In this context, Quentin Skinner wrote the famous book *Meaning and Understanding in the History of Ideas,* which can be interpreted as a blistering critique of the method of historians Lewis Namier and Geoffrey Elton.

Namier considered ideology to be a distortion of reality. In his view, the historian should investigate the real motives that led to political acts. He believed that historians of the intellectual current were naïve for taking the speeches of historical agents seriously[7].

Elton also believed that intellectual history was outside of real life and that historical research should be carried out mainly by consulting manuscript archives and private writings.

Skinner, in a completely opposite direction, sees ideology as a fundamental element in understanding history. Influenced by Max Weber, Skinner believes that ideologies function as enablers. Political agents, therefore, could only proceed with their actions if their ambitions were constructed in such a way as to be considered legitimate by their interlocutors.

The great texts, which until then were considered to be timeless and could solve problems from very different periods from those in which they were written, were relativized and had to be seen according to the context of the time in which they were written. In his *Foundations*, Skinner presents a more pragmatic and less mythical view of the classics.

Another aspect that permeates Skinner's works is the use of less conventional sources, such as the works of diplomats, theologians, jurists, artists and

---

[7] GOLDIE, Mark. The context of The Foundations. In: BRETT, Annabel; TULLY, James. **Rethinking the Foundations of Modern Political Thought**. Cambridge: Cambridge University Press, 2002, p. 5.

writers. Such use brings History closer to other social sciences, a fact that was criticized by historians of ideas.

The question of language is another controversial issue that Skinner addresses in his works. He argues that it is necessary to know the author's intention and reconstruct the context in which the text was written in order to really understand its meaning, which is therefore related to its use.

In addition, Skinner uses Collingwood's logic of question and answer to affirm that every text must be understood as a response to specific problems of a given time .[8] Texts, therefore, are not timeless. Since they are not timeless, it is necessary to find out why the author wrote the text.

In this context, the fundamental notions of context and agency emerge, that is, the discovery of the question to which the text is an answer and the act of the authors who are responding to particular situations and other specific texts.[9].

Wittgenstein had a real influence on the thinking of the Cambridge school, as he propagated a philosophy of language that suited the desires of Cambridge historians. According to the philosopher, it is not possible to think of words as simply names of objects, but rather through their use in language. Therefore, in order to understand a concept, one must understand how the author is using words to discuss it, through contextual analysis of the other possible uses of these words.

J.L. Austin was another author who influenced Skinner. The concepts of locutionary act and illocutionary act were widely used in *Foundations* to underpin the methodology of the Cambridge school. The locutionary act is simply saying something, unrelated to any other type of action. The illocutionary act, *contrario sensu*, refers to how a speech is used, *e.g.* to warn, to demand something, to censure, to criticize. The illocutionary act, therefore, is essential for understanding discourse, as it serves to determine the force of words[10]. From another perspective, if a politician wants his speech to be understood by the audience, he must adapt it to the linguistic

---

[8] HAMILTON-BLEAKLEY, Holly. Linguistic philosophy and The Foundations. In: BRETT, Annabel; TULLY, James. **Rethinking the Foundations of Modern Political Thought**. Cambridge: Cambridge University Press, p. 5
[9] *Ibidem,* p. 23.
[10] AUSTIN, J.L. **How to Do Things with Words.** Oxford: Oxford University Press, 1962, p. 132.

and social conventions of the time in which it is delivered.

Skinner's work has been well received by several authors, but many historians criticize the method used by him and his colleagues at the Cambridge School. Particular mention should be made of the criticism made by conceptual history authors, who point out various inconsistencies in the methodological project of the Cambridge School. In response to these provocations, Skinner went so far as to affirm the impossibility of a conceptual history, believing that each concept has a single existence in the work of a certain author .[11]

Joao Feres Junior makes a strong criticism of the Cambridge school, claiming that Skinner wrongly applied the theory of speech acts to written texts. Feres Junior states that it is not possible to consider spoken discourse to be identical to textual discourse, as text has various characteristics that differentiate it from orality.

Paul Ricoeur identified these characteristics, dividing them into: temporal flow, references, linguistic code and communication[12]. Oral discourse is necessarily present and does not extend into the future, while writing causes discourse to be fixed and live on in posterity. Speech is self-referential, because the author speaks directly to the interlocutors. Text, on the other hand, is referenced. The linguistic code used is different and communication is established directly in oral discourse, while it is carried out mediately, through the text, in writing.

Illocutionary acts, therefore, partially lose their comprehension through inscription. It is not possible to observe intonation or gestures and other resources used in discourse when we are in front of a text. Completely reconstructing the author's intention through textual analysis becomes a thankless task, if not completely impossible.

Skinner still believes that it is possible to reconstruct the author's intention by studying his biography and historical context, but he doesn't go into detail about how it is possible to be sure that a given meaning was what the author intended for his readers.

[11] FERES JUNIOR, Joao. From Cambridge to the World, Historically: Reviewing Quentin Skinner's Methodological Contribution, **Revista de Ciencias Sociais**, Rio de Janeiro, Vol. 48, n°3, 2005, p. 676.

[12] *Ibidem,* p. 667.

Finally, Joao Feres Junior states that: "the journey to the past must follow a journey back to the present"[13]In other words, the understanding of a text must not remain linked only to the meaning of a past era (if it can be reconstructed), but must be valid today.

It is inconceivable that the situation of the interpreter and the time in which he is inserted should be disregarded. Texts expose themselves to the interpretation of new readers, who constantly change the old meanings because of their own worldview: this is the phenomenon of reception, which Collingwoodians tend to ignore because they believe that this theory, which comes from literature, is not applicable to history. They are wrong, according to Feres Junior, because they underestimate the valuable methodological contributions of literature to History.

1.3 The project of a Conceptual History for Brazil

There are currently countless Conceptual History projects around the world. They all consist of attempts to adapt the *Begriffsgeschichte* to local, regional, continental or even transcontinental realities, as is the case with the Ibero-American project.

In Brazil, the main historian who has tried to develop a well-defined project with application to Brazilian history is Joao Feres Junior. The author is widely celebrated in academic circles and is one of the big names in the school of conceptual history.

Brazil has a number of particularities that make the task somewhat complex, since the countless ruptures, periods of crisis, the various constitutions and the discontinuity of governments cause constant changes in the concepts that prevail in society and in the use of them.

Before focusing strictly on the national project, however, Feres Junior criticizes the notion of key concepts in the *Begriffsgeschichte.* This definition states that, in order to be considered key concepts, terms must be the scene of political contestation and conflict. Feres Junior argues that the study of counter-concepts is also important, since uncontested concepts can play an important role in the oppression and

[13] *Ibidem,* p. 672.

exclusion of individuals and groups in a society[14].

As an example of a counter-concept, he presents the term *Latin America,* which was created to act as a counter to the concept of America. The term was used in a pejorative way, to indicate that there was a difference between the America of the United States and the rest of the continent. Even though it has a certain continuity, it is possible to assimilate some modifications in its meaning and scope.

Regarding the adaptation of the history of concepts to the Brazilian reality, Feres Junior proposes an analysis that takes into account the triple problem that Brazilian society is currently facing, namely problems of a socio-economic, political-institutional and political-cultural nature.

The main socio-economic problem is the country's poor income distribution, despite being one of the largest economies on the planet. The political-institutional problem refers to the consolidation of liberal democracy. The politico-cultural problem concerns the Brazilian belief that the country is part of the West, with values and culture similar to Europe, while Europeans and Americans consider the country to be an exotic, non-Western land.[15].

In order to deal with the aforementioned problems, it is necessary to build a national project for the history of concepts that is guided by the following guidelines: I) Adoption and institutional consolidation of the republican-democratic regime. II) The construction of a Brazilian national identity. III) Brazil's economic and demographic revolution in the 20th century.[16].

The first guideline is to study the evolution of the republican regime in Brazil, following the legal and political debates and analyzing fundamental concepts such as democracy, freedom, political rights and the constitution, among others.

The second guideline deals with the study of the formation of a national consciousness since the Proclamation of the Republic, focusing on concepts of Brazilianness, national interest and others derived from cultural movements that

[14] FERES JUNIOR, Joao. Towards a critical conceptual history of Brazil: welcoming the *Begriffgeschichte.* In: FERES JUNIOR, Joao (org.); JASMIN, Marcelo (org.). **Historia dos conceitos**: dialogos transatlanticos. Rio de Janeiro: PUC Rio, Loyola, IUPERJ, 2007, p. 114.

[15] *Ibidem,* p. 115.

[16] *Ibidem,* p. 115.

sought to nationalize foreign art and literature, such as anthropophagy and luso-tropicalism.

Finally, the third guideline emphasizes the importance of analyzing demographic change in the 20th century. Internal migratory phenomena should also be studied. Fundamental concepts in this context are negro, black, mulatto, favela and others.

The Brazilian conceptual history project is still in progress and may undergo important modifications until it is accepted by the academic community in general as a well-founded and adapted method for explaining Brazilian history.

1.4 Global History and David Armitage

Soon after the end of the Second World War, an effort was made to promote cooperation between peoples, with the aim of achieving greater integration and avoiding wars. This effort included the creation of the UN and its specialized agencies, including UNESCO (United Nations Educational, Scientific and Cultural Organization).

At the beginning of the 1950s, UNESCO began an ambitious project to write the history of humanity, focusing on the various cultural interactions between peoples, the points of contact between their histories, the reciprocal influences; in short, to write a true history of globalization.

Entitled *History of Mankind,* the project was to be carried out in disregard of the prevailing Eurocentric and ethnocentric views and could not privilege one specific region over others[17]. In this context, the theory of Global History emerged, a history constructed by all peoples and which could not disregard the external influences suffered by nations.

The UNESCO project experienced a number of difficulties, especially considering that the systemic context at the time was the Cold War. Turner, an American and one of the main historians involved in the project, had to deal with the

---

[17] DUEDAHL, Poul. Selling Mankind: UNESCO and the Invention of Global History, 1945-1976, **Journal of World History**, Honolulu, Vol. 22, n. 1, p. 101.

entry of the Soviets from 1954.

After Stalin's death and Krushev's rise to power, the Soviet Union decided to become a member of UNESCO and closely monitor the project to build a global history. Zvorikine, the Soviet representative, did not initially propose any significant changes to the project, but as soon as the manuscript of the first volume was ready, the Soviets wrote a huge critique, proposing so many changes that it was necessary to postpone the publication of the initial volume in order to analyze the relevance of the criticisms.

After decades, the volumes of *History of Mankind* were published, but they did not have a wide repercussion among historians, partly because the attempt to bring together historians from all over the world, with different ideas, to produce a definitive work on the history of mankind failed, partly because the delay in publication made the work obsolete and distant from the main historiographical currents of the time .[18]

The value of the work, however, is that it is the first truly global project for the construction of history and that it emphasizes the importance of studying cultural interactions between peoples as a way of truly understanding a country's history.

Today, the study of Global History is once again gaining prestige in academic circles. David Armitage, departing from the Cambridge School and Conceptual History, argues that both schools fail to concern themselves with the international dimension in the study of history. In a critique of Quentin Skinner's *Foundations*, Armitage[19] states that: "Yet, save for a brief but suggestive account of neo-scholastic conceptions of the law of nations, *Foundations* included no treatment of the state in its nature, its powers or its rights as an international actor."[20]

We can therefore see the importance of studying the international dimension in historical analysis. It is no longer possible to isolate the borders of a state and believe that the isolated study of that country's history is sufficient for an accurate

---

[18] *Ibidem,* p. 102.

[19] ARMITAGE, David. Hobbes and foundations of modern international thought. In: BRETT, Annabel; TULLY, James. **Rethinking the Foundations of Modern Political Thought**. Cambridge: Cambridge University Press, p. 219.

[20] "However, except for a brief but suggestive explanation through neo-scholastic conceptions of international law, *Foundations* did not include the treatment of the State in its nature, its powers or its rights as an international actor" (our translation).

historical analysis.

Armitage argues that historical and political analysis in its international dimensions is not a recent phenomenon, but appears as early as Hobbes, who can be considered as the first realist theorist of international relations[21]. For the author, Hobbesian theory is among the three traditional theories of international relations, alongside Hugo Grotius' theory of international solidarity and Kant's international society.

The study of history, especially political history, is expanding to include international, global and cosmopolitan aspects[22] . Redefining the frontier of the history of political thought seems to be one of the main tasks of the historian of the 21st century.

Having begun his study of global history through the study of Atlantic history, Armitage has attracted increasing attention to his project. He argues that those who don't explicitly study history in its international or global dimension should justify themselves, because it has been proven that transnational connections have played an important role in the history of humanity since its inception[23].

Armitage's major work, written from a global perspective, is *Declaration of Independence: A Global History,* in which he analyzes the impact of the United States' Declaration of Independence on the world and the external influences on the drafting of the document.

In the United States, the declaration is basically interpreted as a charter of fundamental rights for citizens. This hermeneutic perspective, however, ignores the real purpose of the document, which was to declare that the United States was no longer part of British colonial rule and was now an independent state. According to the language of diplomacy used at the time, a declaration was a formal international pronouncement by an official body, by means of a general manifesto or communiqué to each state[24].

---

[21] *Ibidem,* p. 220.

[22] *Ibidem,* p. 235.

[23] ITTERSUM, Martine; JACOBS, Jaap. Are we all global historians now? An interview with David Armitage, **Itinerario**, Cambridge, Vol. 36, 2012, p. 16.

[24] ARMITAGE, David. **Declaration of Independence: a global history.** Translated by Angela

At the time the declaration was drafted, people from various countries took part in the process, including the British and the Irish.[25]. The declaration was influenced, albeit partially, by the Dutch Act of Abjuration, in which the States General publicly expressed their repudiation of the authority of King Philip of Spain, stating their reasons for doing so.[26]This was like the third part of the declaration of independence of the United States.

Regarding the declaration's impact on the international scene, it served as a model and inspiration for many similar declarations around the world, especially in other American countries. From the time of the declaration, several colonies rebelled against their metropolises and founded independent states, as can be seen from the number of independent countries that emerged in the first decades of the 19th century.

This example shows the importance of studying history from a broader perspective, both territorially and temporally, in order to fully understand the important events in the past of a people, nation or state.

1.5 The applicability of Global History to the study of amnesty

Before examining the subject of this topic, it is important to present some fundamental concepts that guide the historical study of amnesty, taking into account the historiographical currents discussed above.

The amnesties in Brazil and Argentina took place in a context of transition between dictatorial and democratic regimes. To better understand the transition, it is essential to study the concepts of democracy and dictatorship, their modern use and how they have changed over time.

Democracy, in its classical sense, used in Greek cities in antiquity, was closely related to the idea of political freedom and was carried out directly by the citizens, through the exchange of opinions, debate and political action.

Currently, the concept of democracy refers mainly to the choice of rulers by the people, i.e. representative democracy. In sociological terms, there are two types of

---

Pessoa. Sao Paulo: Companhia das Letras, 2011, p.32.

[25] *Ibidem,* p.17.

[26] *Ibidem,* p.41.

modern democracy: radical democracy, which holds equality as its highest value, and liberal democracy, which holds freedom as its highest value. What they have in common is distrust of rulers, who must be supervised.[27].

Dictatorship, on the other hand, is a term that originated in Ancient Rome and meant the rule of a magistrate, who had a temporary function and was supposed to act in times of war, revolt or administrative chaos. The dictator therefore received his powers from the Senate. Since dictatorship was expressly provided for by law, the dictator acted within the same regime, without causing ruptures[28].

The modern meaning of dictatorship, however, is used in a negative sense, as a political regime as opposed to democracy. Modern dictatorships can be classified into three types: simple, Bonapartist and totalitarian. Simple dictatorships rely on the state's traditional means of coercion to maintain the dictator's power. Bonapartist dictatorships are supported by the people. Totalitarian dictatorships occur when one party controls power, with popular support. What they all have in common is the use of force by the state against nationals and the strengthening of the executive branch, which becomes more important than the other powers[29].

After studying these concepts, it is important to conceptualize our object of study. Amnesty, for criminal law, is a type of grace, "with the purpose of covering up all the criminal characteristics of certain criminally reprehensible acts, by prohibiting criminal prosecution or erasing previously imposed sentences".[30]

According to the original meaning of the word, amnesty, which derives from the Greek amnistia, means forgetting. It is closely associated with forgiveness, but not on the part of the victims, only on the part of the state. Historically, its aim has been to establish social peace in a context of regime transitions.

Amnesty in its penal character and as part of the transition to a democratic regime is a recurring theme in the literature, but many authors ignore the international dimension of the debate. As has already been pointed out, it is not possible to analyze

---

[27] SILVA, Kalina Vanderlei; SILVA, Maciel Henrique. **Dicionario de conceitos historicos**. Sao Paulo: Contexto, 2ª ed., 2006, entry Democracy, pp.89-90.

[28] *Ibidem,* entry on Dictatorship, pp. 106-107.

[29] *Ibidem,* entry Dictatorship, p. 108.

[30] BASTOS, Lucia Elena Arantes Ferreira. **Amnesty**: international laws and the Brazilian case. Curitiba: Jurua, 2009, p. 48.

an event in a country's history in isolation. The international context must be taken into account, which means that the theory of Global History is fully applicable to the study of amnesty.

Brazil granted a broad and unrestricted political amnesty in 1979 and the law is still in force. Argentina, a neighboring country, considered its amnesty laws unconstitutional in 2005, thus allowing criminal prosecution and the disclosure of criminal facts to the victims' families. It is interesting that countries so close geographically have taken such different approaches to the issue.

By comparing the positions of Brazil and Argentina, from the perspective of Global History, we can find the reasons for the discrepancy in understandings. It should be noted that the history of the two countries has been quite different since their independence.

Argentine history has been greatly influenced by expansionist ideals and a strong sense of Americanism. Its independence was even greatly influenced by the declaration of independence of the United States and the French Revolution. Despite being banned, volumes of the Declaration of the Rights of Man, translated into Spanish, arrived in Buenos Aires in cargoes from slave ships.[31]. No wonder the Republic was the form of government chosen by the newly independent country.

Brazil's history, on the other hand, is marked by the maintenance of the *status quo* and, during the imperial period, by relations with Europe, with greater integration with American countries only occurring after the advent of the republic .[32] Brazil's independence, for example, led to the application of the constitutional monarchy model, albeit with peculiarities, having been carried out by the colonial elite.

The differences between the foreign policies of the two nations, from the earliest moments of their histories, are elements that help to understand how each reacts to international pressures and how different cultures, political and even legal, react to the trial of amnesties.

---

[31] PIGNA, Felipe. **1810**: La otra historia de nuestra revolucion fundadora, Buenos Aires: Planeta, 2010, p. 75.
[32] CERVO, Amado Luiz; BUENO, Clodoaldo. **Historia da Politica Exterior do Brasil**, Brasilia: Universidade de Brasilia, 4ª ed., 2012, p.179.

In the following chapters, we will focus on the detailed study of each national situation and how global history can be of great value to the study of amnesty.

2 AMNESTY IN BRAZIL

2.1 Historical context

Before beginning the analysis of amnesty itself in Brazil, we need to understand the context in which the law was enacted, i.e. the transition from military rule to democracy. In order to investigate the reasons for the breadth of the Amnesty Law, one must go back to the 1964 coup and bring up a brief history of the dictatorial period.

In 1964, the world was going through moments of tension as tempers flared over the Cold War. The possibility of a third world war between the two superpowers was feared: The Soviet Union and the United States. A war of such magnitude that it could destroy the planet.

In Brazil, the situation was also tense, as President Joao Goulart made speeches that were interpreted by Udenist politicians as communist in nature. The re-establishment of diplomatic relations with the USSR caused panic in the most conservative sectors of society and a certain distrust in the United States.

Until the JK government, Brazil's alignment with the capitalist bloc reduced the country's room for maneuver on the international stage, but from Janio Quadros onwards, the doctrine of Independent Foreign Policy was established. What Janio used as a bargaining tool ended up contributing to the fall of Joao Goulart, who was seen as a leftist by the US government. The United States was therefore ready to supply arms and fuel to the rebellious military and could help in the event of a conflict. It was called Operation *Brother Sam,* which ended up being canceled due to the rapid resolution of the impasse[33].

It is not possible, however, to attribute the 1964 movement exclusively to US aid, given the nationalist nature of the military discourse. Thus, on March 31, 1964, the military took power in Brazil. The military governments were marked by the Institutional Acts, decrees that sought to strengthen the regime and restrict civil and political rights. Because of their importance, we will briefly discuss the first five

[33] *Ibidem,* p.389.

Institutional Acts (AI) and their impact on Brazilian politics.

In the very first days, AI-1 was published, suspending parliamentary immunities, authorizing the "command of the revolution" to revoke mandates at any level, among other measures. AI-2 established indirect elections for the President of the Republic and extinguished the existing political parties. AI-3 established indirect elections for state governors. AI-4 convened Congress to approve a new constitution (1967). The infamous AI-5 corresponded to an escalation of the dictatorship, through censorship of the media, suspension of the right to *habeas corpus* for those accused of crimes against national security, the economic and social order and the popular economy, among other measures[34].

It is now important to briefly consider each military government and how the alternation between the hard-line generals and those in favor of a gradual return to democracy was carried out, as well as to elucidate aspects of the conflict between the regime and its opponents.

The Castelo Branco government was characterized by an attempt to establish a kind of "restricted democracy"[35]aimed at putting an end to the "communist threat" and corruption. Castelo believed in a peaceful transition to a right-wing democratic government. He was perceived, however, as being too lenient with his opponents.

In 1967, Castelo was unable to succeed him and the hardline military and authoritarian nationalist group managed to elect General Artur da Costa e Silva. His government was marked by the beginning of the armed struggle and the further closure of the regime. At this time, the National Liberation Alliance (ALN) and other opposition groups emerged, advocating armed struggle to end the military regime, inspired by the success of the Cuban Revolution. AI-5 and the national information system also emerged, systematizing torture within the regime.

After suffering a stroke, Costa e Silva was unable to continue as President. The military ministers, however, did not want the vice-president to take over because he had opposed AI-5. The solution, therefore, was to create a junta, by means of AI-

---

[34] FAUSTO, Boris. **History of Brazil**. Sao Paulo: Universidade de Sao Paulo, 14ª ed., 2012, p. 409.
[35] *Ibidem,* p.401.

12, to govern the country. From this brief period, we can highlight the kidnapping of the American ambassador by opponents, the creation of the banishment sentence and the emergence of the DOI-Codi (Detachment of Operations and Information and Center for Internal Defense Operations), major torture centers of the military regime .[36]

General Emilio Garrastazu Medici was elected president after Costa e Silva was unable to recover. Medici's government was characterized by the height of repression. At the time, propaganda was very strong about the Brazilian economic miracle, a period in which GDP growth averaged 11% a year, which was unprecedented in Brazilian history. There were also gigantic construction projects, such as the Rio-Niteroi bridge. The fear of torture and death kept opponents quiet, except for the Araguaia guerrilla movement, in which the government transformed the region into a national security zone and liquidated the movement.

Medici, however, failed to elect his successor and General Ernesto Geisel was chosen as president. He began to open up the regime towards democracy. Some measures stand out, such as the suspension of censorship and the end of AI-5. However, there were several reactions to the opening up, including the famous case of the death of journalist Vladimir Herzog, who was murdered inside the DOI-Codi in Sao Paulo, although the government's version was that he had committed suicide[37].

One movement that characterized the period of transition to democracy was Operation Condor. Through this operation, the CIA was supposed to help in the fight against communism in Latin America[38] . In Brazil, it supplied weapons and encouraged attacks that would be attributed to the left. Violent strategies were used to combat re-democratization[39].

On the practice of torture and cruel crimes within the dictatorship, police officer Claudio Guerra's memoir provides us with a meticulous account of the practices and the ways in which the crimes were concealed. He tells us about a

---

[36] *Ibidem,* p. 411.
[37] *Ibidem,* p. 419.
[38] ABRAMOVICI, Pierre. **The nightmare of "Operation Condor"**. Available at: http:// www.diplomatique.org.br/acervo.php?id=401 Accessed on: 01. Oct. 2013
[39] GUERRA, Claudio; NETTO, Marcelo; MEDEIROS, Rogdrio. **Memories of a dirty war**. Rio de Janeiro: Topbooks, 2012, p. 130.

specific crime:

> According to my companions, Colonel Perdigao then unleashed all his sadism. I was told that the moga, Ranusia, although wounded, managed to get out of the car before the fire, unlike her three companions, who ended up charred. She was in a bad way, in agony. It was Perdigao who made a point of shooting her to death. And he laughed as he shot. He laughed out loud.[40]

We can see that there was a certain cruelty in the crimes committed by the dictatorial government. These crimes continued to occur during Geisel's administration, despite the talk of a path towards redemocratization through a slow, gradual and secure opening. Among the authoritarian measures of the Geisel government, the "April package" stands out, which created the figure of the bionic senator to prevent the MDB (Brazilian Democratic Movement) from having a majority in the Senate[41].

Geisel succeeded his successor, General Joao Batista Figueiredo. His government was characterized by economic problems and a deepening of the military regime's openness. At the time, international interest rates were rising and there was little foreign investment. The government then turned to the IMF, which imposed austerity measures that did not please the population.

On the political front, the Amnesty Law was passed by Congress. This was one of the opposition's traditional demands. However, the amnesty was very broad, covering even the torturing agents of the military regime, which generated a strong debate about its validity. This debate continues to this day and will be the subject of the next few pages.

After the Figueiredo government, Tancredo Neves was elected, albeit indirectly, and it was the opposition's first victory since 1964, marking the end of the military dictatorship.

2.2 Justiga de Transigao in Brazil

Justice of Transition is a concept developed by the United Nations Security

---

[40] *Ibidem,* p. 47.
[41] FAUSTO, Boris. *Op. Cit,* p.420.

Council, which encompasses four practices for dealing with the reminiscences of regimes of exception: reforming institutions for democracy, the right to memory and truth, the right to reparation and adequate legal treatment of crimes committed under authoritarian rule.

There are currently several models of transitional justice around the world. Whether after military dictatorships, as in the Latin American cases, or after civil war, as in the former Yugoslavia, or even in the South African case of Apartheid, there is a need to resolve outstanding problems by means of a balanced solution, which is not revanchist, but which does not ignore the suffering of the victims and their families.

The International Center for Transitional Justice (ICTJ) is an organization present in several countries, including Brazil and Argentina, to assist in the transition process and build civil trust in state institutions as guarantors of human rights, as well as partnering with civil society groups seeking truth and accountability for abuses committed during the regime of exception.[42].

In Brazil, the transitional justice model adopted is somewhat complex. Because of the theoretical impossibility of criminally punishing the guilty parties, due to the Amnesty Law and the paradigmatic judgment of the Supreme Court (see section 2.4), the Brazilian government has adopted a system of civil liability, establishing indemnities to compensate for the moral and material damage suffered by the victims and their families.

As a step forward in the attempt to revisit the past, mention should be made of the creation of the National Truth Commission in 2011, which aims to clarify the facts and circumstances of serious human rights violations, including identifying those responsible. The commission does not, however, have a jurisdictional or prosecutorial nature. Its focus is on clarifying the truth and reconstructing collective memory.

In December 2014, the commission delivered a three-volume report on human rights violations committed by the military regime[43] . The first volume deals with the history of the National Truth Commission, domestic and international

[42] INTERNATIONAL CENTER FOR TRANSITIONAL JUSTICE. **Our Work**. Available at: <http://www.itcj.org/our-work> Accessed on: Apr. 10, 2017

[43] NATIONAL TRUTH COMMISSION. Home page. Available at: http://www.cnv.gov.br Accessed on: 10 Apr. 2017.

repressive structures, with a specific chapter on Operation Condor and collaboration between authoritarian regimes in Latin America. Volume II deals with specific themes, such as violations of the rights of indigenous peoples, violations in universities and civil society's resistance to human rights violations. The last volume deals with the political dead and disappeared, a fundamental topic for clarifying the fate of the regime's victims. Because of the scope of this work, the subject will not be explored in depth, since our focus is on studying amnesty in Brazil.

The commission was inspired by the South African model. In that country, the Truth and Reconciliation Commission guaranteed broad participation by the accused, who were not concerned with defending themselves, but only with clarifying the facts in order to obtain a pardon. As a result, it was relatively simple to achieve full disclosure of what happened, including uncovering those who benefited *from apartheid*, such as agricultural companies, mining companies, the war industry and some investors.[44].

However, the mere existence of a truth commission and its report does not exclude the possibility of discussing the Amnesty Law and seeking accountability.
of those accused of committing human rights violations. Some argue that accountability in the criminal sphere is better than the existence of truth commissions, because the accused actively participates in the trial, contributing to their reintegration into society. Furthermore, the information generated in a trial is more accurate, due to procedural rules and the production of evidence[45].

The advantages of criminal punishment are confronted with practical difficulties and face many controversies. Law 6833/79, by granting amnesty to crimes related to political crimes, would have, according to the dominant interpretation, granted amnesty to the torturers and murderers of the military regime.

There is a stricter interpretation, however, which believes that related crimes must affect the same legal asset and have an ideological, consequential or occasional link with the main crime, forming a criminal unit. For adherents of this

---

[44] NEVES, Raphael. A Truth Commission in Brazil? Challenges and prospects for integrating human rights and democracy. **Lua Nova**, Sao Paulo, v. 86, 2012, p. 179.

[45] *Ibidem,* p. 176.

current, the torturers were never granted amnesty, because they had a different objective from defying the prevailing political system, since the torturers' function was to ensure the *status quo* and eliminate resistance to the regime.[46]The interpretation that would consider the torture and murders practiced by military agents as crimes related to political crimes is unjust.

Amnesty is a form of extinguishment of punishability. Thus, for those who believe that the military were amnestied, it is impossible to punish them criminally, not least because Law 6833/79 would have been accepted by the Federal Constitution of 1988 and the concept of political crime would depend on the interpreter's view and could be questioned. For this current, the preservation of the State is also a political motivation and should be included in §1 of art. 1 of the Amnesty Law. Those who defend this interpretation believe that a more restrictive interpretation would violate the principle of the non-retroactivity of criminal law to the detriment of the defendant[47].

Swensson Junior believes that the only possibility of punishment in the criminal sphere is through the application of the Radbruch Formula[48]. According to Radbruch, when justice is not even intended and equality is consciously denied in the act of creating laws, the law is not only "unjust law", but lacks a legal nature[49] . This formula was used at the Nuremberg Tribunal to punish the Nazis responsible for crimes against humanity.

Another controversial issue is the validity of the Amnesty Law, which is that the military amnestied themselves (self-amnesty). The question therefore arises as to the possibility of such an amnesty, which should have come into force after broad discussion and participation by civil society, which was left out of the process.

---

[46] BASTOS, Lucia Elena Arantes Ferreira. **Amnesty**: international laws and the Brazilian case. Curitiba: Jurua, 2009, p. 194.

[47] SWENSSON JUNIOR, Lauro Jopert. Punishment for the crimes of the military dictatorship: outlines of the debate. In: et al. **Justi^a de transi^ao no Brasil**. Sao Paulo: Saraiva, 2010, p. 40.

[48] *Ibidem,* p. 48.

[49] RADBRUCH, Gustav. Gesetzliches Unrecht und ubergesetziches Recht (1946). In: Rechtsphilosophie. Stuttgart: Koehler, 1973 p. 345-346 *apud* SWENSSON JUNIOR, Lauro Jopert. Punishment for the crimes of the military dictatorship: outlines of the debate. In: et al. **JustRa de transi^ao no Brasil**. Sao Paulo: Saraiva, 2010, p. 48.

Going back to when Law 6833/79 was drafted, there was an initial intention to exclude the so-called "terrorists", i.e. those who took part in the armed struggle against the military regime, from amnesty .[50] The original meaning of oblivion, inherent in the term amnesty, was recalled many times in the preliminary draft of the law, with the prevailing idea being that amnesty should bury the dictatorial regime, erasing all human rights violations that took place during the period.

Furthermore, the 1979 amnesty maintained the tradition of several previous amnesties in Brazil's history. The amnestied military personnel were initially only the top names in the Armed Forces, with sailors and some military personnel with leftist tendencies suffering discrimination, as they were not reinstated to their previous positions . There was even an Association of the Military Not Completely Amnestied (AMINA).[51].

The amnesty, however, was extended by the 1988 Constituent Assembly. The amnesty period was also extended from September 18, 1946 to the date of the promulgation of the Constitutional Charter. It can be seen, therefore, that even among the military, the Amnesty Law was not very well received, since, in practice, it excluded several lower-ranking military personnel.

Once Law 6833/79 has been studied, other pieces of legislation related to transitional justice need to be analyzed. Law 9140/95 (Law of the Disappeared) grants family members the right to request death certificates for victims of the military regime and to receive compensation. Although it represented a breakthrough, the law fails to place the burden of proof on the relatives themselves, when it is simpler for the state itself to prove the alleged facts[52].

---

[50] SCHINKE, Vanessa Dorneles. **Political amnesty in Brazil:** the indications and misrepresentations of the discourse of oblivion in the light of the discursive theory of law and democracy. Supervised by Professor Menelick de Carvalho Netto, Brasilia, 2009. 108 f. Dissertation (Master's in Law) - University of Brasilia, Postgraduate Program in Law, Area of Concentration: Law, State and Constitution. Brasilia, 2009, p. 24.

[51] DA CUNHA, Paulo Ribeiro. The military and amnesty in Brazil. In: TELES, Edson; SAFATLE, Vladimir. **What remains of the dictatorship**: the Brazilian exception, Sao Paulo: Boitempo, 2010, p. 32.

[52] MEZZAROBA, Glenda. The process of settling accounts and the logic of arbitrariness. In: TELES, Edson; SAFATLE, Vladimir. **What remains of the dictatorship**: the Brazilian exception, Sao Paulo: Boitempo, 2010, p. 111.

Another breakthrough was Law 10559/02, which deals with obtaining the status of political amnesty, as well as the compensation to be received by victims or their families. Shortly before the law came into force, the Amnesty Commission was set up in the Ministry of Justice, which has to analyze the requests for compensation made by those who were prevented from working for political reasons .[53]

It can be seen that the analysis of Brazilian amnesty is quite complex, due to the many controversial issues, the difficulty of reaching a compromise between the parties and the definitive resolution of the issue, since the debate is fertile, new ideas emerge all the time and the argument that was considered right becomes questionable.

2.3 Amnesty Law in the face of international law

International human rights law is today one of the main branches of international law and is constantly expanding. In order to guarantee the effectiveness of its norms, the UN created a global protection system through the Universal Declaration of Human Rights of 1948 and the International Covenants on Civil and Political Rights and on Economic, Social and Cultural Rights, both of 1966.

The global system, however, is still somewhat vulnerable, as it does not have many structures capable of imposing sanctions on states that fail to comply with multilateral agreements.[54]. Furthermore, there is no body with a jurisdictional function responsible for identifying human rights violations and punishing those responsible.

To complement the global system, various regional human rights protection systems have emerged, such as the European system, the Inter-American system, the African system and there are tendencies towards the emergence of an Asian system. These systems are not intended to replace the global protection established by the UN, but to strengthen it based on the specific characteristics of each continent.

The inter-American system emerged from the Organization of American States (OAS), which was created as a result of the Pan-Americanist ideal of forming a more integrated American continent. The system's main bodies are the Inter-American Commission on Human Rights and the Inter-American Court of Human Rights. The

---

[53] *Ibidem,* p. 112.

[54] COELHO, Rodrigo Meirelles Gaspar. **International protection of human rights**: the Inter-American Court and the implementation of its rulings in Brazil. Curitiba: Jurua, 2008, p.49.

main norm is the 1969 American Convention on Human Rights, which came into force in 1978.

Not all OAS member states have ratified the American Convention. The United States and Canada can be mentioned as notable absentees[55]. These states are only committed to the OAS Charter and the American Declaration of Human Rights and are not subject to the jurisdiction of the Inter-American Court. Brazil ratified the Convention in 1992 and acceded to the contentious jurisdiction of the Court in 1998, with the exception of complaints of human rights violations that occurred before the recognition of the Convention.[56].

The Inter-American Court has both an advisory function (on the interpretation of the Convention) and a jurisdictional function (judging cases in which the Convention has been violated by one of the states that have acceded to its jurisdiction). Individuals, however, cannot submit a claim directly to the Court, but must act through the Inter-American Commission, which will make a kind of prior judgment on the admissibility of the claim.

Brazil has already suffered a number of condemnations before the Court, one of the most emblematic being the case of Gomes Lund ("Guerrilha do Araguaia") *v.* Brazil. Human Rights Watch and the Center for Justice and International Law filed a petition with the Inter-American Commission on behalf of people who disappeared during the Araguaia Guerrilla (see section 2.1.1). The Commission then submitted the case to the Court.

As one of its preliminary objections, the Brazilian state argued that the Court had no jurisdiction to judge human rights violations that took place before Brazil's accession to contentious jurisdiction in 1998. Some authors argued that the Court had no jurisdiction either to judge events that took place during the military dictatorship or to annul the Brazilian Amnesty Law .[57]

The Court, however, partially rejected the preliminary ruling on the grounds

---

[55] MAZZUOLI, Valerio de Oliveira. **Course in Public International Law**. 6.ed. Sao Paulo: Editora Revista dos Tribunais, 2012, p. 897.

[56] *Ibidem,* p. 905.

[57] SWENSSON JUNIOR, Lauro Jopert. Punishment for the crimes of the military dictatorship: outlines of the debate. In: et al. **Justiga de transRao no Brasil**. Sao Paulo: Saraiva, 2010, p. 44.

that enforced disappearances of persons are continuous and remain so until the facts are properly clarified or the individuals are found.[58]. The preliminary ruling was only accepted in relation to the extrajudicial execution of a woman who had her remains identified in 1996, that is, two years before Brazil recognized the Court's contentious jurisdiction.

On the merits, the judges upheld the request and ordered the Brazilian state to conduct a criminal investigation into the facts of the case in order to clarify them and punish the perpetrators. Brazil must also do its utmost to find the missing persons, carry out a public act of acknowledgement of international responsibility, typify the crime of forced disappearance of persons, among other measures[59].

With regard to the Amnesty Law, the Inter-American Court considered it to be incompatible with the American Convention and to have no legal effect. The judges affirmed that Law 8633/79 cannot continue to be an obstacle to investigating and punishing those responsible for human rights violations during the military dictatorship.

The Brazilian government, however, doesn't seem to care about the Inter-American Court's ruling, as the Amnesty Law continues to produce its effects, having been deemed constitutional by the Federal Supreme Court in a recent judgment (see topic 2.4).

If the law is invalid before the inter-American system, it is also invalid before the global human rights protection system, because the crimes committed during the military dictatorship can be considered crimes against humanity.

The precise concept of crimes against humanity emerged after the Second World War, a historic event that impressed the world with its practices of extreme cruelty and abuse. Article 6(c) of the Statute of the Nuremberg Tribunal provides a very broad concept of crimes against humanity, including murder in certain situations.

In order to be considered a crime against humanity, the crime must characterize a particularly repulsive offense, be part of a government policy or consist of a systematic practice that is not adequately sanctioned by the government, be a

[58] INTER-AMERICAN COURT OF HUMAN RIGHTS. Case of Gomes Lund et al. v. Brazil, judgment of November 24, 2010, Serie C n° 219, p.10.

[59] *Ibidem*, p. 115.

prohibited act, regardless of whether in wartime or peacetime, and the victims must have been civilians.[60]. It can be seen that the crimes committed under the military regime have the characteristics mentioned above.

Crimes against humanity, by their very nature, are imprescriptible. Imprescriptibility is provided for in a specific convention (1968 Convention on the Imprescriptibility of War Crimes and Crimes against Humanity) and is part of international *jus cogens*, i.e. it is an ineradicable rule of general international law, recognized by the international community of states as a whole, which can only be modified by a subsequent rule of general international law of the same nature, as provided for in art. 53 of the 1969 Vienna Convention on the Law of Treaties.

Finally, it should be noted that the main human rights treaties converge on the prohibition of torture . [61]The 1984 UN Convention against Torture and Other Cruel, Inhuman or Degrading Treatment or Punishment was recently elevated to the status of international *jus cogens*. Brazil ratified the convention, including permission to be monitored internationally. In the Convention, there is an obligation to prosecute and punish torturers, and victims must be guaranteed the right to judicial protection[62].

It is clear that Brazil is failing the international community by using the shield created by Law 6833/79 to try to absolve itself of the responsibility of bringing torturers and human rights violators to justice, as well as feeding a feeling of discredit towards the judicial institutions and the Brazilian government among its citizens.

2.4 The Supreme Court's decision on the constitutionality of the Amnesty Law

In 2010, an ADPF (Argument for Non-Compliance with a Fundamental Precept) reached the Brazilian Supreme Court, discussing the constitutionality of the Amnesty Law (Law 6683/79). The action was filed by the Federal Council of the OAB (Brazilian Bar Association) to question the content of §1 of art. 1 of the Amnesty Law. See the content of this provision:

---

[60] BASTOS, Lucia Elena Arantes Ferreira. **Amnesty**: international laws and the Brazilian case. Curitiba: Jurua, 2009, p. 54.

[61] PIOVESAN, Flavia. International human rights law and the amnesty law. In: TELES, Edson; SAFATLE, Vladimir. **What remains of the dictatorship**: the Brazilian exception, Sao Paulo: Boitempo, 2010, p. 97.

[62] *Ibidem,* p. 98.

> **Art. 1** - Amnesty is granted to all those who, in the period between September 2, 1961 and August 15, 1979, committed political crimes or crimes related to them, electoral crimes, those who had their political rights suspended and civil servants of the Direct and Indirect Administration, of foundations linked to the public power, civil servants of the Legislative and Judicial Powers, military personnel and union leaders and representatives, punished on the basis of Institutional and Complementary Acts.
>
> **§ Paragraph 1 - For the purposes of this article, crimes of any nature related to political crimes or committed for political reasons are considered related:!**

In the initial petition, the council's lawyers want the STF to interpret the aforementioned §1 in accordance with the Constitution, because the current interpretation would directly violate the fundamental precepts and principles present in the Constitutional Charter, such as the dignity of the human person (art. 1, III), legal equality (art. 5, *caput* and XXXIX) and the democratic and republican principles (art. 1, *caput).* Furthermore, they argue that the wording of the provision in question is intentionally obscure, to allow the inclusion of those who committed violations of fundamental rights in the name of the dictatorial regime[63].

They also argue that the question of connection must be analyzed through the concepts of formal and material competition, in the case of a single agent, or connection when agents act against each other. In the latter case, however, the rule is purely procedural in nature and there must be a unification of jurisdiction.

Finally, the Council asks the Supreme Court to declare that the amnesty granted by Law 6683/79 does not extend to common crimes committed by agents of the military regime against political opponents.

Initially, questions were raised about the admissibility of the lawsuit, since according to the Attorney General's Office (AGU) there was no judicial controversy that would authorize the use of ADPF. Another requirement that had not been met, according to the AGU, was that there had been no challenge to the entire complex of legislation governing the issue, given that §1 of article 4 of Constitutional Amendment 26/1985 also grants amnesty for political and related crimes.

---

[63] BRAZIL. Supreme Federal Court. Arguigao de Descumprimento de Preceito Fundamental n° 153/DF, Relator Ministro Eros Grau, Brasilia DF, April 26, 2010. **Diario da Justiga Eletronico**, no. 145, published on 06/08/2010.

The Attorney General's Office, on the other hand, argued that the case should be heard because, for the purposes of an ADPF, it is sufficient for there to be a constitutional controversy, and judicial controversy is not necessary. Furthermore, Article 4 of EC 26/85 did not replace, ratify or alter the provisions of the Amnesty Law. It argues that the alleged statute of limitations for the crimes cannot be an obstacle to analyzing the merits of the ADPF. On the merits, it opines that the request should be dismissed.

The STF justices, almost in their entirety[64]rejected the preliminaries raised by the AGU, on the grounds that there was a relevant constitutional controversy and that there was no other effective judicial measure of constitutionality control for the case in question.

The case was then referred for judgment, with Justice Eros Grau as rapporteur. By 7 votes to 2, the ADPF was dismissed. We must now analyze the vote of the rapporteur, who rejected the request, and the vote of Justice Ricardo Lewandowski, who diverged from the prevailing view.

Justice Eros Grau begins his argument by distinguishing between text and norm. According to the minister, the norm is only produced after the text has been interpreted, and then the phenomenon of the concretization of the law occurs. The justice argues that the ADPF is questioning the legal text itself and not the norm, since it would be the text itself that would be infringing isonomy.

He went on to say that the right to receive information from public bodies, guaranteed in Article 5, XXXIII of the Federal Constitution of 1988, was not violated by the Amnesty Law, since the law does not at any time prohibit access to historical documents. For such access to be granted, there are other legal provisions to be challenged.

As for the offenses against the democratic and republican principles, the minister says that the argument is not sustainable, as it disregards the phenomenon of constitutional reception, in which previous norms can be incorporated into the new constitutional order. The fact that the amnesty was voted on in a Congress controlled

[64] With the exception of Justice Marco Aurelio, who took the view that the case should be dismissed without judgment on the merits, as there was no procedural interest.

by the military, according to Eros Grau, would not be enough to annul the Amnesty Law, and a referendum or a new vote by democratically elected representatives would be unnecessary to legitimize the law.

As for the dignity of the human person, the minister argues that the argument is merely political and not legal, given that the principle enshrined in art. 1, III of the CF/88 could not have been contradicted before it came into force. He argues that the fight for amnesty is being forgotten by the Applicant, recalling that the OAB itself defended amnesty and was committed at the time to the enactment of the law. The illustrious magistrate even states that the OAB, by disregarding this struggle, would be incurring *in venire contra factum proprium*[65]. He concludes this point by stating that the argument does not hold water. With respect to the minister, the fight for amnesty was never intended to benefit agents of the military government, but only the regime's political opponents.

After countering the alleged violations of fundamental precepts, the judge went on to analyze the possibility of interpretation in accordance with the constitution. The justice states that the connection provided for in Article 1, Paragraph 1 of the Amnesty Law is *sui generis*, as it was drawn up at a time of transition to democracy, and even covers the military in charge of repression. The amnesty, in the minister's words, was certainly bilateral.

The STF's case law on previous amnesties in Brazil's history was to reaffirm that they also covered related crimes, always to the benefit of the defendants. The interpretation was therefore broad and generous, considering the political and legal purposes of the amnesty.

He continues his analysis by presenting the concept of laws-measures, which regulate certain interests and are concrete and immediate, unlike other laws, which are abstract and have effects that last over time. Measure laws would therefore be laws in the formal sense, but not in the material sense. Such laws should be interpreted in accordance with reality and the historical moment in which they were enacted. At the time it was drafted, the amnesty for agents of the military regime was

[65] BRAZIL. Supremo Tribunal Federal, **Op. Cit.**, p. 22.

already condemned by the international community.

For the minister, the Amnesty Law is a measure law and it is impossible to interpret it according to the values of contemporary society. Since it is a law-measure, the impossibility of granting amnesty for torture (art. 5, XLIII of CF/88) and the UN Convention against Torture and Other Cruel, Inhuman or Degrading Treatment or Punishment, which came into force in June 1987, would not apply to the Amnesty Law, which was prior to it and would already have had its effects. I strongly disagree with the position adopted, since if the Amnesty Law continues to prevent access to justice for those who have suffered human rights violations or their families, it cannot be considered a law-measure.

Eros Grau concludes by saying that the Supreme Court cannot change the text of a law, which is reserved for the Legislative Branch. Not even to repair profound injustices could the Supreme Court act as if it were a legislator. He briefly compares Brazil's compromise process with its South American neighbors (a rather superficial comparison, which disregards the role of the Argentine Supreme Court), stating that a new law is needed to revoke the political agreement that granted amnesty. The amnesty would have been accepted by the Constitution, even because it was included in EC 26/85. He concludes by dismissing the case.

In the opposite direction is the vote of Justice Ricardo Lewandowski, who ruled partially granted the request. The magistrate began his speech by recalling the context of widespread popular rejection of the military regime at the time when the Law of Amnesty was enacted. It mentions the protests that took place abroad, through governments and international organizations, such as Amnesty International.

Quoting Thomas Hobbes, the Justice says that the interpretation of the provision under analysis must be made by examining the will of the law, and not that of the legislator, based on more objective hermeneutic criteria. He lists the types of connection present in Brazilian law to conclude that none of them are applicable to §1 of art. 1 of the Amnesty Law, since there is no unity of will or conduct between the agents.

The crimes committed by the military would be crimes against humanity (including under the Nuremberg Statute, ratified by Brazil in 1945) and would also fall under various criminal types present in the Penal Code at the time of the regime of exception. Torture, even without this nomenclature, was never admitted in the Brazilian Republic, and the conduct could be classified as bodily harm or ill-treatment. The minister also uses international humanitarian law to state that, even in a state of war, certain ratified international standards must be respected.

He goes on to state the need to apply the concept of political crime present in the STF's jurisprudence, developed mainly in extradition reviews. A pure political crime is one that affects the personality of the state, or seeks to alter or affect its political or social order. The impure political crime, on the other hand, generates a legal injury of a common nature[66]. The Supreme Court's jurisprudence also differentiates violent crimes committed against the person (known as "blood crimes") from other political and related crimes, by adopting the criteria of prevalence and atrocity of the means. Violent crimes were treated as common in the extradition cases judged by the Supreme Court, on the grounds that to authorize the punishment of the political enemy illegally would be to return to the Hobbesian state.

For Justice Lewandowski, the approach to impure political crimes should be carried out on a case-by-case basis and not abstractly, through the aforementioned criteria. He states that the defects present in the Amnesty Law continued to be present in EC 26/85 and that it is not possible to disregard Article 5 (XXXV) of the Federal Constitution of 1988 (access to justice).

Finally, he recalls the duty to investigate and punish in various international standards, such as the Covenant on Civil and Political Rights and the American Convention on Human Rights. In the operative part, the minister grants an interpretation in accordance with the Constitution, understanding that the amnesty for the military was not automatic and establishes a case-by-case approach, according to the preponderance and atrocity of the means, in order to determine whether the crime was related or not.

Despite the lucidity of Justice Ricardo Lewandowski's vote, the majority of the Justices followed the rapporteur, deciding that the ADPF should be dismissed, maintaining the current interpretation and the validity of Law 8633/79. The decision upheld Brazil's tradition of impunity, causing much dissatisfaction among human

[66] *Ibidem*, p. 119.

rights activists and the international community, as since 2001 the UN has been pressuring the Brazilian government to repeal its Amnesty Law .[67]

Trying to discover the reasons that led to the strange model of transitional justice adopted by Brazil, European historian Nina Schneider analyzes in an article the STF decision as an element that represents the lack of interest of Brazilians in the subject, since only 40% of the population in 2010 was in favor of punishing human rights violators[68]according to a Datafolha poll. She concludes that the STF missed a precious chance to strengthen human rights in Brazil and end the process of transition to democracy.

The writer is correct in her analysis. There is also the complete lack of knowledge of international law on the part of Brazilian magistrates as a complicating factor in the justice of compromise in Brazil.

Contrary to its external actions, in which Brazil is a well-known respecter of international norms and even an agent of transformation, in the internal sphere it remains stuck in unnecessary formalisms, which undermine the credibility of institutions and the letter of the law, which can still be considered a remnant of the military dictatorship, which encouraged ufanism and the prevalence of internal law.

The Attorney General of the Republic, Rodrigo Janot, stated in an opinion on extradition that Brazilian amnesty must be subject to the international conventions ratified by Brazil and that crimes against humanity are, in fact, imprescriptible[69]. Justice Marco Aurelio, commenting on the issue, stated that: "yesterday's Supreme Court was one, today's is another"[70] , pointing to the possibility of the STF changing its understanding of amnesty. The outcome of the recent changes of position in the debate on the justice of compromise in Brazil must be awaited.

---

[67] SCHNEIDER, Nina. Impunity in Post-Authoritarian Brazil: The Supreme Court's Recent Verdict on the Amnesty Law. **European Review of Latin American and Caribbean Studies**, Amsterdam, v. 90, pp. 39-54, April 2011, p.50.

[68] *Ibidem,* p. 45.

[69] ARRUDA, Roldao. Attorney General challenges Amnesty and says torture and death are imprescriptible. **O Estado de Sao Paulo**, Sao Paulo, October 18, 2013, Politica.

[70] BULLA, Beatriz. STF to re-discuss Amnesty if provoked, says Marco Aurelio. **Agencia Estado**, Sao Paulo, October 21, 2013, Politica. Available at: <http://www.estadao.com.br/noticias/nacional,stf-rediscute-anistia-se-for-provocado-diz-marco-aurelio,1088112,0.htm> Accessed on: 03 Nov. 2013.

In 2014, the PSOL (Socialism and Freedom Party) proposed ADPF 320[71]which questions the effects of the Amnesty Law. The party asks that the law not be applied to agents of the military regime who committed serious human rights violations. It argues that the judgment of the Inter-American Court has not yet been complied with. For the time being, the case has not yet been heard, meaning that the retrograde understanding that prevents the criminal liability of agents of the military regime prevails.

71 BRAZIL. Federal Supreme Court. **PSOL questions the effects of the Amnesty Law.** Available at: http://www.stf.jus.br/portal/cms/verNoticiaDetalhe.asp?idConteudo=267078 Accessed on: 10 Apr. 2017.

3 AMNESTY IN ARGENTINA

3.1 Historical context

For the purposes of this paper, it is essential to study the last military dictatorship that took place in Argentina (from 1976 to 1983). Understanding the period, however, depends on a prior understanding of the unstable past of Argentine politics, which is why we need to look at Argentine history in a broader context.

Argentina's history has been characterized by several authoritarian periods. From 1930 to 1983, the country had only two constitutional rulers who completed their terms in office. The year 1930, in fact, is a watershed in Argentine history. From 1860 to 1930, the country was one of the richest in the Americas and had great influence in South America. Some of the factors that enabled Argentina's development at the time were the strong presence of European immigrants and the growth of the export economy .[72]

The years following the crisis of 1929 had a strong impact on the Argentine economy and allowed for the installation of authoritarian governments. Among them was that of populist leader Juan Domingo Peron, elected in 1946. Peron's government was characterized by income redistribution through the strengthening of state protection for workers[73]. His wife Evita was a true national icon, loved by the workers. The Peronist government, however, suffered a coup in 1955.

Between 1955 and 1966, the Argentine state was governed alternately by civilians and the military. In 1966, General Juan Carlos Ongania overthrew the elected government to establish a regime similar to the Brazilian military dictatorship[74] , based on the famous National Security Doctrine, according to which the state of exception was necessary to contain the communist threat. A notable movement at the time was the "Cordobazo", which brought together workers and students to protest against the policies of the Ongania government. This movement laid the foundations for the urban guerrillas.

---

[72] WRIGHT, Thomas C. **State Terrorism in Latin America**: Chile, Argentina and International Human Rights. Lexington: Roman & Littlefield Publishers, 2007, p. 95.

[73] *Ibidem,* p.96.

[74] *Ibidem,* p.97.

The main guerrilla movements were the *Ejercito Revolucionario del Pueblo* (ERP) and the *Montoneros.* The latter had a strong Peronist inspiration and believed that only the return of Peron could save Argentina from moments of instability. The growth of the urban guerrillas in the early 1970s and, in particular, of the Montoneros group, strengthened the popular clamor for the return of the former populist leader.

Peron was elected president in 1973, but his attitudes greatly disappointed the guerrillas. Despite granting amnesty to those who took part in the armed struggle, the Peronist government cracked down hard on left-wing agendas, especially those of the ERP. Its minister Jose Lopez Rega created the dreaded AAA *(Alianza Anticomunista Argentina),* which functioned as a death squad to eliminate left-wing guerrillas .[75]

When Peron died in 1974, his widow Isabel Peron took over the presidency. Isabel's government was a prelude to the dictatorial period that followed. She authorized "Operation Independence", aimed at eliminating a popular uprising in the province of Tucuman[76]. The operation led to the creation of the first secret detention center, where many people were tortured and murdered.

On March 24, 1976, there was a new military coup, which did not surprise the population, already accustomed to the lack of continuity in Argentine politics. The new government is promptly recognized by the United States and even receives support from the International Monetary Fund.[77].

The military governments were guided by a program: the National Reorganization Process. This idea is so striking that the period is known as "el Proceso". Basically, the process consisted of putting an end to the urban guerrillas and exterminating any spark of opposition. Jacobo Timerman[78], who had been a political prisoner, goes further, stating that: "World War III had begun; the enemy was left-

[75] MIGUENS, Marcela Siqueira. **Transitional justice in the Latin American context:** its characteristics, foundations and a comparison between Brazil and Argentina. Supervised by Professor Carlos Eduardo Adriano Japiassu, Co-supervised by Professor Rodrigo de Souza Costa, Rio de Janeiro, 2011. 175 f. Dissertation (Master of Laws)- State University of Rio de Janeiro, Postgraduate Program in Law, Area of concentration: Public Law. Rio de Janeiro, 2011, p. 98.

[76] WRIGHT, Thomas C, *Op. Cit.,* p. 98.

[77] MIGUENS, Marcela Siqueira. *Op. Cit,* p. 99.

[78] WRIGHT, Thomas C, *Op. Cit.,* p. 105.

wing terrorism; and Argentina was the initial battleground chosen by the enemy".[79]. The idea of putting an end to the red menace was present in military discourse and practice.

Power in the dictatorial regime was exercised through military juntas, which were made up of the general commanders of the army, navy and air force. There were several juntas during this period, the most famous of which was the first, made up of Jorge Rafael Videla, Ramon Agosti and Emilio Eduardo Massera .[80] Videla was chosen as the nation's president. Argentina was divided into security zones to facilitate military control.

The regime established power through terror, torture, murder and, above all, the disappearance of individuals.[81]. Disappearance was a particularly cruel strategy, as it did not allow the victim's relatives to know the fate of the missing person, feeding false hopes within the family. It was, however, very effective, as the bodies did not turn up to incriminate the government.

Another repeated practice was the creation of secret detention centers, some of them in the capital itself. One of the centers was located in the basement of Galerias Pacifico, a traditional shopping area in downtown Buenos Aires. The prisoners could even hear the noise from the street .[82] A frequent and terrifying practice were the death flights, in which people were thrown from airplanes into the Atlantic Ocean.

In order to combat these practices and denounce the abuses of the regime, various organizations emerged to defend human rights. The best-known movement was the *Madres de Plaza de Mayo*, which was started in April 1977 by mothers who wanted information about their disappeared children[83]. They stood in front of the presidential palace protesting. From modest beginnings, the movement grew to become one of the best-known human rights organizations in the world, and even had

---

[79] The Third World War had begun; the enemy was left-wing terrorism; and Argentina was the first battlefield chosen by the enemy" (our translation).

[80] MIGUENS, Marcela Siqueira. *Op. Cit.* , p. 99.

[81] The ICTJ (International Center for Transitional Justice) claims that between 10,000 and 3,000 people disappeared during the dictatorial period in Argentina. On the subject, see LICHTENFELD, Rebecca. **Accountability in Argentina**: 20 Years Later, Transitional Justice Maintains Momentum. New York: ICTJ Case Study Series, 2005, p.8.

[82] WRIGHT, Thomas C, *Op. Cit.*, p. 110.

[83] *Ibidem,* p. 120.

connections with foreign media.

International pressure also began to mount on the regime, which took a risk by hosting the 1978 World Cup, because the international press was interested in finding out whether human rights violations were actually taking place. The government, however, knew how to hide its trail of crimes very well.

The tide began to turn when then US President Jimmy Carter demanded a visit by the Inter-American Commission on Human Rights to Argentina in exchange for the US government supplying equipment for the construction of a dam. The commission's report confirmed the human rights violations and stated that they were not only committed against guerrillas[84].

In order to contain the growing questioning, the Argentine government launched a bold military campaign: the Falklands War in 1982. The islands were traditionally claimed by Argentina, but had been under British rule since the 19th century. The hope of the military was that the war would unite them around a common purpose and strengthen the regime. It was also believed that the British would be slow to act and that the United States would remain neutral, due to the anti-communist struggle in Argentina .[85] The US government, however, supported the British, who won the war, causing national humiliation and inevitably leading to the end of the dictatorship.

Another factor that helps explain the downfall of the dictatorship is the economy. In the years from 1976 to 1983, the resources allocated to social welfare were reduced and the share of wage earners in national income fell progressively[86]. The strategy of deindustrializing certain regions didn't work either. In addition, Argentina suffered from the foreign debt crisis, when interest rates were unilaterally increased by the US Federal Reserve.

All these factors combined, the military regime came to an end in 1983, when Raul Alfonsin, a candidate for the UCR (Union Civica Radical del Pueblo) was

---

[84] *Ibidem,* p. 124.
[85] CANDEAS, Alessandro Warley. Brazil-Argentina relations: an analysis of advances and setbacks. **Revista Brasileira de Polftica Internacional,** Brasilia, v. 48(I), pp. 178-213, 2005, p. 24.
[86] QUINTAR, Aida; ARGUMEDO, Alcira. Argentina: the dilemmas of restricted democracy. **Lua Nova,** Sao Paulo, n° 49, pp. 35-63, 2000, p. 37.

elected president, promising to defend human rights and penalize the military for its excesses.

3.2 Justiga de Transigao in Argentina

Argentina can be considered a model of transitional justice for the world. Although it has oscillated between impunity and accountability, by opting for the latter, the country has made great strides towards the definitive resolution of the transition to democracy and the consolidation of the democratic regime.

Soon after he was elected, Alfonsin sought to repeal the decree in which the military granted amnesty, through a bill that was approved by Congress[87]. Another key initiative was the creation of the National Commission on the Disappearance of Persons (CONADEP), which was tasked with investigating all cases of forced disappearance that occurred during the dictatorship. The commission was criticized for its limited powers, since it could not investigate other human rights violations, such as torture, homicide and others.

CONADEP produced the report *Nunca Mas,* in which it noted the disappearance of 8,960 people and the existence of 340 clandestine detention centers[88]. Inside these centers, conditions were precarious and detainees were subjected to various types of humiliation. The report also reported that thousands of people had been murdered and their bodies destroyed to hinder the investigation. In addition, CONADEP drew up a list with the names of 1351 repressors. The report finally contradicted the military version that the killings were just excesses in the war against subsidization.

The commission was one of the first of its kind and was widely copied by several countries around the world. In South America, Chile, Uruguay, Peru and others followed the commission model. On other continents, Nigeria, East Timor and South Africa are some of the countries that have followed Argentina's example[89].

---

[87] WRIGHT, Thomas C, *Op. Cit.*, p. 142.

[88] CUYA, E. Justiga de Transigao. **Revista Acervo**, Rio de Janeiro, v.24, n° 1, pp.37-78, 2011, p. 50.

[89] WRIGHT, Thomas C, *Op. Cit.*, p. 146.

CONADEP's work, however, did not sit well with the military, who were in favor of completely forgetting the past. They even tried to prevent a television channel from broadcasting the *Nunca Mas* report by throwing an explosive on the station's roof.[90]

As well as setting up CONADEP, Alfonsin called for the trial of the main leaders of the military regime and certain members of the guerrillas. In 1984, the trial took place, considered a milestone in Latin American judicial history[91] . The Supreme Council of the Armed Forces had jurisdiction to try the case. The reform of the Military Justice Code, however, expressly authorized the transfer of the case to a civilian court if the Council was negligent or delayed the trial. This is what happened in this case, and the case was heard by the Federal Court of Appeal in Buenos Aires.

The defense argued that human rights violations were nothing more than collateral damage of a just war against subversion[92]. The argument, however, was not considered and two members of the first junta, Videla and Massera, were sentenced to life imprisonment. The trial acted as a response to demands for justice and served to reassure the population that justice would be done.

The military were angry and restless at the large number of cases opened over human rights violations after the paradigmatic trial of members of the first junta .[93] In several situations, the military simply refused to obey court orders from civilian magistrates.

To appease tempers and prevent another coup, in 1986 Alfonsin enacted the *Ley de Punto Final (Final Point Law),* which set a time limit of 30 days for the publication of new accusations and 60 days to start legal proceedings. Although this was a victory for the impunity of the military, they were still not satisfied. They even rebelled in Campo de Mayo, the country's largest military base[94].

President Alfonsin was forced to submit another bill to Congress that would

---

[90] CUYA, E. *Op. Cit.,* p. 51.

[91] VASCONCELOS, Daniela. Authoritarianism, human rights and redemocratization: a comparative analysis of transitional justice in Brazil and Argentina. **Revista Andina de Estudios Politicos**, Lima, Vol. III, n° 1, pp.134-165, 2013, p. 148.

[92] WRIGHT, Thomas C, *Op. Cit.*, p. 149.

[93] VASCONCELOS, Daniela, *Op. Cit.*, p. 149.

[94] WRIGHT, Thomas C, *Op. Cit.*, p. 155.

extend the impunity of the military. The *Ley de Obediencia Debida,* enacted in June 1986, exempted all military personnel from lieutenant colonel to the bottom of the hierarchy from criminal responsibility, on the grounds that those who followed orders were merely following military directives and respecting the chain of command. In the next section, we'll see how fallacious this argument is. In practice, only a very few individuals could be held responsible.

The situation was further complicated when an attack on a military base near Buenos Aires, known as *La Tablada*, killed 40 soldiers and left at least 100 injured[95]. The attack was blamed on a guerrilla group, which weakened the human rights movement and increased military suspicions that human rights organizations were a front for leftist terrorism.

The newly elected president, Saul Menem, aiming to establish national reconciliation, issued several pardons to human rights violators, including former junta members such as Videla, Massera and Agosti.[96]. Several guerrillas were also pardoned. The only advance in terms of transitional justice at that time was the establishment of reparations for the victims. The mere granting of financial compensation did not please some organizations, such as the *Madres de Plaza de Mayo.*[97].

In the mid-1990s, however, the situation began to change. With the end of the military uprisings and the strengthening of international human rights law, the possibility of punishing those who violated fundamental rights returned to the fore. Argentine society began to mobilize on the issue once again.

An important event in 1995 was the creation of HIJOS *(Hijos por la Identidad y la Justicia y contra el Olvido y el Silencio).* Initially brought together to share the pain of having their parents disappeared during the military regime, they quickly expanded and increasingly turned their meetings towards politics . [98]They

---

[95] *Ibidem,* p. 156.

[96] VASCONCELOS, Daniela, **Op. Cit.**, p. 150.

[97] WRIGHT, Thomas C, **Op. Cit.,** p. 158.

[98] RUA, Santiago Cueto. HIJOS de victimas del terrorismo de Estado. Justice, identity and memory in the human rights movement in Argentina, 1995-2008. **Historia Critica**, Bogota, n° 40, pp.122-145, 2010, p. 131.

became known for their *escraches,* in which they went to the homes of dictatorship repressors to shame them and challenge their impunity. The *escraches* were a way of punishing the repressors, who couldn't be legally punished[99].

The judiciary began to hold some human rights violators accountable by arguing that the kidnapping of children was not included in the amnesty laws. In 1998, Videla and Massera were arrested. International human rights organizations began to monitor the situation in Argentina and even foreign governments, such as Spain and Italy, investigated disappearances of their nationals in Argentina .[100]

In 2001, federal judge Gabriel Cavallo ruled that the final point and due obedience laws were unconstitutional. Despite fears that the Argentine crisis would damage the movement to end impunity, the continued search for truth and justice was intensified by the arrival of Nestor Kirchner, who had been persecuted by the military regime.

Finally, in 2005, the Supreme Court upheld the lower court's decision and ruled that the laws of due obedience and period are unconstitutional, paving the way for the definitive criminal liability of those accused of committing human rights violations and confirming international jurisprudence, setting an example to be followed.

3.3 Amnesty laws in the face of international law

Despite not expressly using the term amnesty, the Final Point and Due Obedience laws were intended to exempt agents who had committed serious human rights violations from responsibility. Since they were enacted, the two laws have been absolutely incompatible with international law, both in the global aspect of human rights protection and in the regional aspect.

The military in Argentina believed they were fighting a war against subversion, with torture and death being merely collateral damage in order to achieve a supposedly noble goal. In this context, they had to obey the military hierarchy and

[99] *Ibidem,* p. 137.
[100] WRIGHT, Thomas C, *Op. Cit.*, p. 167.

respect orders from their superiors. This was even one of the foundations of the Law of Due Obedience. However, even in wartime, there are minimum standards of conduct to be respected.

In order to combat abusive practices during periods of war, international humanitarian law emerged, developing mainly after the end of the Second World War. The main rules of this branch of international law can be found in the Geneva Conventions of 1949. The importance of this new legal discipline was emphasized by the Nuremberg Tribunal, which was responsible for making it possible to punish war criminals in an international court.

Article 8 of the Charter of the Nuremberg Tribunal states that compliance with an order issued by a superior cannot exempt the person who carried it out from responsibility. Such an order would only serve as a factor in reducing the accused's sentence.

The order, however, must be manifestly illegal. To have this characteristic, the command must be so contrary to the law that it does not arouse any kind of doubt in the subordinate as to its illegality[101]. In practice, the illegality of the order will be analyzed on a case-by-case basis.

To really be able to use such a line of defense, the subordinate must have had doubts about the legality of the order, or use compliance with the order as part of a defense alleging coercion. If the accused did not know and had no way of knowing that the order carried out was illegal, he cannot be held responsible[102].

It is clear that the crimes committed during the Argentine military dictatorship, abstractly considered, were committed in full awareness of the illegality of the orders. Complying with orders from hierarchical superiors, therefore, cannot be accepted as a justification for committing the crimes, which *in itself* would make the Law of Due Obedience invalid under international law.

As for the Final Point Law, the principle of access to justice in relation to international crimes is enshrined in international law, i.e. victims have the right to see

---

[101] SOLIS, Gary D. **The law of armed conflict**: international humanitarian law in war. New York: Cambridge University Press, 2010, p. 359.
[102] *Ibidem,* p.358.

those who have committed international crimes prosecuted.[103]. As this law constitutes an obstacle to the application of the principle, it is also invalid under international law.

Furthermore, the crimes committed by the Argentine military dictatorship, as well as the crimes committed by the regime of exception in Brazil, are crimes against humanity. The most up-to-date definition of what is required for a crime to have this characteristic is found in article 7 of the Statute of the International Criminal Court, which states:

> "For the purposes of this Statute, "crime against humanity" shall mean any of the following acts, when committed as part of a widespread or systematic attack against any civilian population, with knowledge of such attack: a) **Homicide**; b) Extermination (...) e) Imprisonment or other severe deprivation of physical liberty in violation of fundamental rules of international law; f) **Torture**; (...) i) **Tornado disappearance of persons**;"- emphasis added

It is clear from reading the provision that there is no doubt about the nature of the crimes committed during the Argentine military regime as crimes against humanity. The fact that the country was not at war (which would contradict Argentina's own military discourse) would not change the nature of the crimes, since crimes against humanity can be committed in times of war or peace[104].

Because they are crimes against humanity, a theory has developed in international criminal law that the subject of these crimes is humanity itself, which makes it possible to try such crimes not only in international courts, but also in the national courts of any country.[105]. National courts would therefore act as representatives of the international community. This is the principle of universal jurisdiction. It should be noted that acts committed in another country by nationals of that other state can be tried in a foreign court.

The principle of universal jurisdiction was used by Spain to issue an international search and seizure warrant for former Chilean dictator Pinochet, who was

---

[103] CRYER, Robert. International Criminal Law. In: MOECKLI, Daniel; SHAH, Sangeeta; SIVAKUMARAN, Sandesh. **International Human Rights Law**. New York: Oxford University Press, 2010, p.553.

[104] *Ibidem,* p.547.

[105] NTOUBANDI, Faustin Z. **Amnesty for Crimes against Humanity under International Law**. Leiden: Martinus Nijhoff, 2007, p. 189.

in London for a visit to Margaret Thatcher in 1998. He was arrested on charges of torture, terrorism and genocide.[106].

In the inter-American system, the case of *Barrios Altos v Peru* consolidated the understanding that amnesties for international crimes are invalid. In the face of all the international and domestic pressure, Argentina decided to annul its amnesty laws, believing them to be incompatible with the Constitution and international law.

3.4 The Argentine Supreme Court's ruling on the unconstitutionality of amnesty laws

The *Supreme Court of Justice of the Nation* had the opportunity to examine the constitutionality of amnesty laws in June 2005, through the Julio Hector Simon case. In this case, a couple and their 8-month-old daughter were kidnapped by the military in 1978, and the child was adopted by the military officer Ceferino Landa. The child was registered under another name, but several pieces of evidence showed that she was indeed the missing child. Her grandmother then decided to go to court to ensure that those responsible for the crimes against her family were punished.

The judge of first instance, when analyzing the case, condemned the military officer Julio Hector Simon, responsible for the torture of the couple, and considered article 1 of the Final Point Law and articles 1, 3 and 4 of the Due Obedience Law to be unconstitutional, for being incompatible with the American Convention on Human Rights, the American Declaration of Human Rights, the International Covenant on Civil and Political Rights and the object and purpose of the Convention against Torture and Other Cruel, Inhuman or Degrading Treatment or Punishment.

The crimes committed by this military officer were considered crimes against humanity and were especially cruel, as they lasted more than a month and involved the constant use of violence, through cruel methods of torture.

After the trial, the defendant appealed to the *Federal Criminal and Correctional Appeals Chamber,* which upheld the sentence, confirming the

[106] WRIGHT, Thomas C, *Op. Cit.*, p. 202.

unconstitutionality of laws 23.492 and 23.521. Given the impossibility of reversing the situation through the ordinary channels, a federal extraordinary appeal was filed, which took the case to the Supreme Court.

The appellant's argument is based on the alleged illegitimacy of the intervention of Horacio Verbitsky, president of CELS (Center for Legal and Social Studies) at the time. He argues that Horacio's participation meant the consecration of a popular action, which would not be appropriate in this case. It also claims that Law No. 23.521 is valid and that the constitutionality of amnesty laws is not an issue that can be debated by the judiciary. It also invokes damage to various criminal guarantees, such as *nullum crimen nulla poena sine lege, the* prohibition of retroactive criminal law and states that it is not possible to relativize constitutionally established guarantees on the basis of norms that constitute *jus cogens*.

The Supreme Court, by seven votes to one, decided to partially uphold the case and declared the Final Point and Due Obedience laws unconstitutional. Justice Enrique Santiago Petracchi reported the case. It is now time to analyze the arguments used by the justices in their judgment.

Justice Petracchi began his speech by stating that the Law of Due Obedience was seriously flawed, as it did not meet the requirement of generality required of the legislative function. Even so, the aim of the law was clear: to grant amnesty for crimes committed during the military regime. Argentine law and international human rights law, however, had undergone several changes over the last few decades.

Since 1994, the hierarchy of international human rights norms has been constitutional, and Argentina has made several commitments to defend human rights, both in the global and inter-American spheres. As far as the Inter-American Court is concerned, the duty of States Parties to guarantee the protection of the fundamental rights of individuals has been enshrined. Within this duty of guarantee, it should be noted that there is a duty to prevent, investigate and sanction the violation of rights guaranteed in the American Convention on Human Rights.

Report 28/92 of the Inter-American Commission on Human Rights highlighted the fact that the amnesty laws violated the rights guaranteed by the

Convention and art. 18 of the American Declaration of the Rights and Duties of Man, which deals with access to justice. The Argentine state had some doubts about the scope of this report, but these uncertainties were resolved through the *Barrios Altos* case, in which Peru was held internationally responsible for its failure to prosecute human rights violations and for having enacted two amnesty laws that prevented the punishment of those responsible for the violations. The Inter-American Court has ruled that amnesties such as the one in this case are inadmissible and violate the American Convention on Human Rights.

The Argentine laws had the same defects as the Peruvian laws, since in both Argentina and Peru the aim of the amnesty laws was to prevent the criminal prosecution of serious human rights violations. Argentina's amnesty laws are therefore notably contrary to international law and should be annulled.

In order to effectively comply with international human rights treaties, therefore, the Final Point and Due Obedience laws would have to be repealed in such a way that there would be no regulatory obstacle to the criminal prosecution of facts such as those in this case, and it would be impossible to invoke the principles of the prohibition of retroactivity of the most serious criminal law and res judicata . [107]Argentina's submission to inter-American jurisdiction would prevent the invocation of these principles, given that serious violations of human rights must be punished.

The minister went on to point out that Congress, in declaring the amnesty laws null and void, by means of Law 25.779, did not remove all the effects of the laws, since it did not make explicit the inapplicability of the principle of the prevalence of the most lenient criminal law.

In the context of the global human rights protection system, the then UN Human Rights Committee published a series of observations on amnesties and concluded that Laws 23.492 and 23.521 are incompatible with the Covenant on Civil and Political Rights. Furthermore, the Committee stated that the rules establishing amnesties should not only be derogated from, but that the derogation should have retroactive effect.

---

[107] ARGENTINA. Supreme Court of Justice of the Nation. Appeal S. 1767.XXXVIII. Cause No. 17.768. Parties: Simon, Julio Hector y otros *vs* Buscarita Imperi Roa. Rapporteur Justice Enrique Santiago Petracchi. Buenos Aires, June 14, 2005, p. 27.

Justice Petracchi concludes his vote by stating that it is not up to the Legislative Branch to declare a law null and void, but to the Judiciary. The final decision, therefore, rests with the judges. Considering it an unnecessary formalism to annul the law that annuls the amnesty and then consider the amnesty null and void, he considers Law 25.779 valid and Laws 23.492 and 23.521 unconstitutional.

Justice Petracchi's vote supported the votes of practically all the justices, but it is important to highlight some arguments that were not used by the rapporteur, regarding the imprescriptibility of crimes against humanity and the *jus cogens* nature of certain norms of international human rights law.

Minister Boggiano points out that the Convention on the Enforced Disappearance of Persons has the character of *jus cogens*, i.e. it is a rule of general international law that cannot be derogated from by any treaty or rule of domestic law. The practical consequence of *jus cogens* is that all nations are obliged to comply with it, even if they did not consent to the drafting of the norm. The Supreme Court has already heard similar cases and ruled that customary international law is part of domestic law. Torture, therefore, has always been an imprescriptible crime, even before the Argentine state ratified the Convention on the Imprescriptibility of War Crimes and Crimes against Humanity.

Justice Maqueda reinforces the idea of *jus cogens* by stating that the 1969 Vienna Convention on the Law of Treaties already expressly provided for the concept of imperative rules of general international law and that, even then, the prohibition of crimes against humanity (which had been defined in the Statute of the Nuremberg Tribunal) had the nature of *jus cogens.*

He ended his vote by pointing out that the traditional principles of criminal law are inapplicable to crimes against humanity, since the aim of this special category of crimes is to punish those responsible wherever they are and regardless of when the crime was committed. Certain restrictions on the punitive power of states would therefore be removed. The more severe nature of the sanctions for these crimes would be due to their seriousness, and it would be imperative to repress them rigorously in order to prevent them from happening again anywhere.

Justice Zaffaroni states that the American Convention was ratified by

Argentina before the amnesty laws came into force, meaning that whatever the criteria used, the Final Point and Due Obedience laws are incompatible with the Convention and should be considered null and void.

The only vote against the unconstitutionality of the amnesty laws was that of Justice Carlos S. Fayt. His arguments, in brief, are as follows: I) The idea of the criminal law of the enemy should not be strengthened, since in a State governed by the rule of law there should be no differentiation between citizens and enemies. II) Fundamental rights and guarantees are inherent to the rule of law and cannot be relativized. III) Constitutional principles of criminal law cannot be considered obstacles. IV) The diffuse and artificial approach of international criminal law cannot lead to the destruction of the liberal principles present in the Argentine Constitution.[108]

It is not possible to agree with the minister's justification, because when the victim is humanity itself, there is no way to make concessions to criminals and only the end of impunity can satisfy the international community. The minister's position, as already stated, was isolated and the amnesty laws were declared unconstitutional.

The decision of the Supreme Court of the Nation has served as a paradigm for transitional justice in Latin America and has demonstrated the value of international human rights law (which underpinned all the favorable votes) and the search for justice, and is an example to be followed by nations that are faltering in resolving the impasse of transitional justice, such as Brazil.

---

[108] ARGENTINA. SUPREME COURT OF THE NATION. *Op. Cit.,* p. 257.

CONCLUSION

The debate about the justice of compromise, whether in Brazil, Argentina, Latin America or other regions of the world, is far from over. There are always those who defend impunity through the granting of amnesties, arguing that impunity is necessary for a peaceful transition and the strengthening of democracy. There are others, however, who believe that it is necessary to review the past and prosecute human rights violators in order to definitively resolve the compromise and strengthen democracy and human rights.

As you can see throughout the book, I am a member of the second camp, because only through trials and Truth Commissions can we achieve true social peace, with the actors of society fully aware of their past and with the punishment of the horrors committed by previous authoritarian regimes, in order to curb possible future violations of the rights inherent to the human person.

The internationalization of law is one of the most discussed phenomena today and it would be a real limitation not to study the influence that international society and even other states have on the context of transitional justice in certain countries, through a comparative study using global history.

As far as this work is concerned, it is impossible not to recognize the influence that the *Barrios Altos* case has had on the Argentine Supreme Court, which even expressly cites the case in the reasoning of its votes and demonstrates a certain concern on the part of the justices about a hypothetical future international liability of the Argentine state.

In the Brazilian case, there was no concern about possible international liability, which in fact occurred months after the STF ruling. The decision was confined to the domestic sphere and did not go into international law or international politics. So far, therefore, Brazil has adopted the model of impunity through amnesty. It should be remembered, however, that the Truth Commission was set up in 2011, reminiscent of the South African model of dealing with the *Apartheid.* In addition, the report published in December 2014 shed light on various crimes and connections that had been hidden by the military.

Some fundamental questions need to be answered and, in order to conclude the work and make it easier to understand, I will analyze them in small sections, formulating my conclusions about the issues.

I) Why has Brazil so far adopted a model of compromise geared towards impunity?

The issue is complex, but I believe that the fact that the Amnesty Law was enacted during the military dictatorship was fundamental to this process. The military, through negotiations with civil society, within the framework of the slow, gradual and secure opening advocated by President Geisel, benefited from the impossibility of being punished for acts committed during the military regime.

In Brazil, the process of breaking with the military regime was not traumatic or sudden. It took a long time for democracy to really return, which meant that the most viable model at the time was the Amnesty Law.

Another contributing factor was the lack of mobilization by civil society against the Amnesty Law and the STF's ruling in ADPF 153. Both national and international human rights organizations, as well as the victims' relatives, were highly critical of the decision, but there were no significant protests or popular commotion on the issue.

One aspect that should also be considered is the relatively small number of victims of the military regime compared to other Latin American countries, such as Argentina .[109] This factor has made the issue of justiga de transigao somewhat abstract for Brazilian society, since undeniably having a relative tortured or killed by repression considerably increases interest in the discussion.

Some say[110] that there are more urgent issues that afflict the Brazilian nation, such as violence, the precariousness of the health system, the poor public basic education system, among others.

The general population's lack of interest in torture victims is also an

[109] SCHNEIDER, Nina. *Op. Cit.,* p.45.

[110] *Ibidem,* p. 45.

important factor. Opponents of the military regime were considered "terrorists" and the general population was in favor of repression. Even today, those who practiced armed struggle against the dictatorship are considered criminals by the most conservative sectors of society, and in their view it is absurd to punish good soldiers who were only defending the nation from external threats, i.e. the infiltration of communists into Brazil. Discourses of this kind are unfortunately gaining strength in the mass media today. The rise of extreme right-wing groups also means that the debate is avoided.

Another factor to be considered is the legalistic tradition of the Brazilian judiciary, in which magistrates believe they are doing the population a service by distancing themselves from the influences of the international community and international law, creating a *sui generis* system of transitional justice, leaving the military unpunished and believing that this is the best thing for Brazilian society.

II) Why has Argentina decided to punish those responsible for serious human rights violations?

First of all, it's worth noting the special relationship that Argentinians have with their past. Unlike Brazil, Argentina takes great care of its historical monuments and the people in general have at least a basic knowledge of the country's history. Proof of this is the beauty of Buenos Aires' historic buildings and the large number of antique shops in the capital.

Attachment to the past keeps the barbarities committed during the last dictatorship alive in Argentinians' memories. The people have not forgotten the horrors to which they were subjected. Furthermore, the number of victims of the dictatorial regime was enormous, one of the largest in Latin America. This has meant that many people are relatives or acquaintances of victims.

Another factor that explains the Supreme Court's decision is the strength of human rights organizations in Argentina. Since the emergence of the *Madres de Plaza de Mayo* and later the *Abuelas de Plaza de Mayo*, the number of organizations fighting for human rights has multiplied. International organizations have also always been vigilant about the Argentine case and have joined forces with national organizations to press for effective punishment of the crimes committed by the military.

Argentine judges also have a good knowledge of international law and don't hesitate to apply it. From very early on in its history, Argentina was influenced by Europe, as many European immigrants came to live in the country, mainly Italians. Not being immune to European legal thinking, the magistrates established a transitional justice system similar to that of many European countries, which sought to ascertain the truth and hold those responsible for serious human rights violations accountable.

In short, Argentina is committed to the punishment model because of its society's own desires and because of effective compliance with international standards on the protection of human rights.

III) Which model of compromise is most effective? Is there really a movement towards accountability in the various models of transitional justice around the world?

On the first question, recent studies show that 40% of the countries that go through transitional justice adopt not just one method, but several.[111]. The main methods are trials, truth commissions, amnesties and monetary reparations. The most successful transitional justice systems have used a combination of trials, truth commissions and amnesties in very limited cases.

It should be noted that the mechanisms can be adopted progressively. Recent studies show that there is generally a standardized procedure in states that adopt a mixed justice system.

Initially, amnesty is granted to ensure a peaceful compromise. After some time, society seeks punishment and trials take place. Pecuniary reparations are only

[111] OLSEN, Tricia D.; PAYNE, Leigh A.; REITER, Andrew G. **Transitional justice in balance**: comparing processes, weighing efficacy. Washington: United States Institute of Peace Press, 2010, p. 105.

adopted after the trials. It is possible to observe that Brazil reverses this order by granting reparations before judging those responsible for crimes against humanity. On this point, it can be considered worthy of praise, as it seeks to provide some form of support to the victims of the previous authoritarian regime. It must, however, complete the process by bringing the criminals of the dictatorial regime to justice.

It can therefore be seen that the most effective model does not stick to a single form of transitional justice, but combines them, dosing the intensity of trials and limiting the scope of amnesties, in order to eliminate the feeling of impunity without creating serious tensions in national society.

With regard to the second question, it is essential to understand the recently created concept of the cascade of justice. The concept serves to affirm that, in the last two decades, countries around the world have chosen to punish human rights violators, unlike the previous period, in which there was a tendency to grant amnesties[112].

This is mainly due to the increase in global and regional action on human rights and the progressive recognition by states of the application and cogent force of international norms by national courts. Other factors contributing to the cascade were the creation of the International Criminal Court and the greater scope and application of the principle of universal jurisdiction[113].

The cascade of justice theory seems to be confirmed by recent data, as it is possible to observe a trend towards criminal responsibility in several countries. Brazil recently seems to be more willing to change the course of its transitional justice towards criminal responsibility.

However, there are those who dispute the theory, believing that the increase in the number of trials is mainly due to the increase in the number of countries that have transitioned to democracy .[114] The increase in the number of truth commissions and the maintenance of the proportion of amnesties would demonstrate, for these scholars, that there is a certain exaggeration in the cascade of justice theory. Exaggeration or not, it is a fact that the number of trials of human rights violators has

[112] *Ibidem,* p. 97.
[113] *Ibidem,* p. 98.
[114] *Ibidem,* p. 101.

increased significantly in the last two decades.

IV) Final remarks

Global history and international law can be used to clarify and contribute to the debate on transitional justice around the world. In the case of Argentina, international law informed the decision of the Supreme Court justices, allowing the criminal liability of the agents of the military regime. The international influence was very clear in the Supreme Court's decision, which also influenced other countries in South America to change their strategy on the issue of transition to democracy.

Brazil, for its part, is still not very open to international influence. Recent events, such as the filing of ADPF 320 by PSOL, however, have raised expectations of a probable change in the STF's position, even to comply with the decision of the Inter-American Court in the Gomes Lund case, in which Brazil was ordered to annul its amnesty laws.

The justice of compromise has always been complex, but it is necessary to face up to the past and deal with it properly in order to strengthen democracy and ensure that traumatic human rights violations never happen again.

REFERENCES

ABRAMOVICI, Pierre. **The nightmare of "Operation Condor"**. Available at: http:// www.diplomatique.org.br/acervo.php?id=401 Accessed on: 01. Oct. 2013

ARGENTINA. SUPREME COURT OF THE NATION. **Recurso de Hecho S. 1767.XXXVIII Simon, Julio Hector y otros s/ privacion ilegitima de libertad, etc. - causa n° 17.768.**

ARMITAGE, David. Hobbes and foundations of modern international thought. In: BRETT, Annabel; TULLY, James. **Rethinking the Foundations of Modern Political Thought**. Cambridge: Cambridge University Press.

. **Declaration of Independence: a global history.** Translated by Angela Pessoa. Sao Paulo: Companhia das Letras, 2011.

ARRUDA, Roldao. Attorney General contests Amnesty and says torture and death are imprescriptible. **O Estado de Sao Paulo**, Sao Paulo, October 18, 2013, Politica.

AUSTIN, J.L. **How to Do Things with Words.** Oxford: Oxford University Press, 1962.

BASTOS, Lucia Elena Arantes Ferreira. **Amnesty**: international laws and the Brazilian case. Curitiba: Jurua, 2009.

BRAZIL. Supreme Federal Court. Arguigao de Descumprimento de Preceito Fundamental n° 153/DF, Relator Ministro Eros Grau, Brasilia DF, April 26, 2010. **Diario da Justiga Eletronico**, no. 145, published on 06/08/2010.

BRAZIL. Federal Supreme Court. **PSOL questions the effects of the Amnesty Law.** Available at: http://www.stf.jus.br/portal/cms/verNoticiaDetalhe.asp?idConteudo=267078 Accessed on: Apr. 10, 2017.

BULLA, Beatriz. STF to re-discuss Amnesty if provoked, says Marco Aurelio. **Agencia Estado**, Sao Paulo, October 21, 2013, Politics. Available at: <http:// www.estadao.com.br/noticias/nacional,stf-rediscute-anistia-se-for-provocado-diz-marco-aurelio,1088112,0.htm> Accessed on: 03 Nov. 2013.

CANDEAS, Alessandro Warley. Brazil-Argentina relations: an analysis of advances and setbacks. **Revista Brasileira de Politica Internacional**, Brasilia, v. 48(I), pp. 178-213, 2005.

CERVO, Amado Luiz; BUENO, Clodoaldo. **Historia da Politica Exterior do** Brasil, Brasilia: Universidade de Brasilia, 4ª ed., 2012.

COELHO, Rodrigo Meirelles Gaspar. **International human rights protection**: the Inter-American Court and the implementation of its rulings in Brazil. Curitiba: Jurua, 2008.

NATIONAL TRUTH COMMISSION. Home page. Available at: http://www.cnv.gov.br Accessed on: 10 Apr. 2017.

INTER-AMERICAN COURT OF HUMAN RIGHTS. Case of Gomes Lund et al. v. Brazil, judgment of November 24, 2010, Series C No. 219.

CRYER, Robert. International Criminal Law. In: MOECKLI, Daniel; SHAH, Sangeeta; SIVAKUMARAN, Sandesh. **International Human Rights Law**. New York: Oxford University Press, 2010.

CUYA, E. Justiga de Transigao. **Revista Acervo**, Rio de Janeiro, v.24, n° 1, pp.37-78, 2011.

DA CUNHA, Paulo Ribeiro. The military and amnesty in Brazil. In: TELES, Edson; SAFATLE, Vladimir. **What remains of the dictatorship**: the Brazilian exception, Sao Paulo: Boitempo, 2010.

DUEDAHL, Poul. Selling Mankind: UNESCO and the Invention of Global History, 1945-1976, **Journal of World History**, Honolulu, Vol. 22, n. 1.

FAUSTO, Boris. **History of Brazil**. Sao Paulo: University of Sao Paulo, 14th edition, 2012.

FERES JUNIOR, Joao. Towards a critical conceptual history of Brazil: welcoming the *Begriffgeschichte.* In: FERES JUNIOR, Joao (org.); JASMIN, Marcelo (org.). **Historia dos conceitos**: dialogos transatlanticos. Rio de Janeiro: PUC Rio, Loyola,

IUPERJ, 2007.

. From Cambridge to the World, Historically: Reviewing Quentin Skinner's Methodological Contribution, **Revista de Ciencias Sociais**, Rio de Janeiro, Vol. 48, n°3, 2005.

GOLDIE, Mark. The context of The Foundations. In: BRETT, Annabel; TULLY, James. **Rethinking the Foundations of Modern Political Thought**. Cambridge: Cambridge University Press, 2002.

GUERRA, Claudio; NETTO, Marcelo; MEDEIROS, Rogerio. **Memories of a dirty war**. Rio de Janeiro: Topbooks, 2012.

HAMILTON-BLEAKLEY, Holly. Linguistic philosophy and The Foundations. In: BRETT, Annabel; TULLY, James. **Rethinking the Foundations of Modern Political Thought**. Cambridge: Cambridge University Press.

INTERNATIONAL CENTER FOR TRANSITIONAL JUSTICE. **Our Work**. Available at: <http://itcj.org/our-work> Accessed on: April 10, 2017.

ITTERSUM, Martine; JACOBS, Jaap. Are we all global historians now? An interview with David Armitage, **Itinerario**, Cambridge, Vol. 36, 2012.

LICHTENFELD, Rebecca. **Accountability in Argentina**: 20 Years Later, Transitional Justice Maintains Momentum. New York: ITCJ Case Study Series, 2005.

MAZZUOLI, Valerio de Oliveira. **Course in Public International Law**. 6.ed. Sao Paulo: Editora Revista dos Tribunais, 2012.

MEZZAROBA, Glenda. The process of settling accounts and the logic of arbitrariness. In: TELES, Edson; SAFATLE, Vladimir. **What remains of the dictatorship**: the Brazilian exception, Sao Paulo: Boitempo, 2010.

MIGUENS, Marcela Siqueira. **Justiga de transigao in the Latin American context:** its characteristics, foundations and a comparison between Brazil and Argentina. Supervised by Professor Carlos Eduardo Adriano Japiassu, Co-supervised by Professor Rodrigo de Souza Costa, Rio de Janeiro, 2011. 175 f. Dissertation (Master of Laws)- State University of Rio de Janeiro, Postgraduate Program in Law, Area of concentration: Public Law. Rio de Janeiro, 2011.

NEVES, Raphael. A Truth Commission in Brazil? Challenges and prospects for integrating human rights and democracy. **Lua Nova**, Sao Paulo, v. 86, 2012.

NTOUBANDI, Faustin Z. **Amnesty for Crimes against Humanity under International Law**. Leiden: Martinus Nijhoff, 2007.

OLSEN, Tricia D.; PAYNE, Leigh A.; REITER, Andrew G. **Transitional justice in balance**: comparing processes, weighing efficacy. Washington: United States Institute of Peace Press, 2010.

PALONEN, Kari. Times of politics and conceptual temporalization: a new program for conceptual history. In: FERES JUNIOR, Joao (org.); JASMIN, Marcelo (org.). **Historia dos conceitos**: dialogos transatlanticos. Rio de Janeiro: PUC Rio, Loyola, IUPERJ, 2007.

PALTI, Elias P Temporality and refutability of political concepts. In: FERES JUNIOR, Joao (org.); JASMIN, Marcelo (org.). **Historia dos conceitos**: dialogos transatlanticos. Rio de Janeiro: PUC Rio, Loyola, IUPERJ, 2007.

PIGNA, Felipe. **1810**: La otra historia de nuestra revolucion fundadora, Buenos Aires: Planeta, 2010.

PIOVESAN, Flavia. International human rights law and the amnesty law. In: TELES, Edson; SAFATLE, Vladimir. **What remains of the dictatorship**: the Brazilian exception, Sao Paulo: Boitempo, 2010.

QUINTAR, Alda; ARGUMEDO, Alcira. Argentina: the dilemmas of restricted democracy. **Lua Nova**, Sao Paulo, n° 49, pp. 35-63, 2000.

RICHTER, Melvin. More than a two-way street: analyzing, translating and comparing political concepts from other cultures. In: FERES JUNIOR, Joao (org.); JASMIN, Marcelo (org.). **Historia dos conceitos**: dialogos transatlanticos. Rio de Janeiro: PUC Rio, Loyola, IUPERJ, 2007.

RUA, Santiago Cueto. HIJOS de victimas del terrorismo de Estado. Justice, identity and memory in the human rights movement in Argentina, 1995-2008. **Historia Critica**, Bogota, n° 40, pp.122-145, 2010.

SCHINKE, Vanessa Dorneles. **Political amnesty in Brazil:** the indications and misrepresentations of the discourse of forgetting in the light of the discursive theory of law and democracy. Supervised by Professor Menelick de Carvalho Netto, Brasilia, 2009. 108 f. Dissertation (Master's in Law) - University of Brasilia, Postgraduate Program in Law, Area of concentration: Law, State and Constitution. Brasilia, 2009.

SCHNEIDER, Nina. Impunity in Post-Authoritarian Brazil: The Supreme Court's Recent Verdict on the Amnesty Law. **European Review of Latin American and Caribbean Studies**, Amsterdam, v. 90, pp. 39-54, April 2011.

SEBASTIAN, Javier Fernandez. Contra la historia (en singular). An interpretation of the work of Reinhart Koselleck. **Ariadna historica. Lenguajes, conceptos, metaforas**, Bilbao, v. 1, 2012.

SILVA, Kalina Vanderlei; SILVA, Maciel Henrique. **Dicionario de conceitos historicos**. Sao Paulo: Contexto, 2ª ed., 2006, entry Democracy, pp.89-90.

SOLIS, Gary D. **The law of armed conflict**: international humanitarian law in war. New York: Cambridge University Press, 2010.

SWENSSON JUNIOR, Lauro Jopert. Punishment for the crimes of the military dictatorship: outlines of the debate. In: et al. **Justi^a de transi^ao no Brasil**. Sao Paulo: Saraiva, 2010.

VASCONCELOS, Daniela. Authoritarianism, human rights and redemocratization: a comparative analysis of transitional justice in Brazil and Argentina. **Revista Andina de Estudios Politicos**, Lima, Vol. III, n° 1, pp.134-165, 2013.

WRIGHT, Thomas C. **State Terrorism in Latin America**: Chile, Argentina and International Human Rights. Lexington: Roman & Littlefield Publishers, 2007.

MIX
Papier aus verantwortungsvollen Quellen
Paper from responsible sources
FSC® C105338

Printed by Books on Demand GmbH, Norderstedt / Germany